UNITED STATES-JAPAN TRADE IN TELECOMMUNICATIONS

Recent Titles in
Contributions in Economics and Economic History

UNITED STATES-JAPAN TRADE IN TELECOMMUNICATIONS

Conflict and Compromise

EDITED BY

Meheroo Jussawalla

Contributions in Economics and Economic History,
Number 145
Dominick Salvatore, *Series Editor*

GREENWOOD PRESS
WESTPORT, CONNECTICUT • LONDON

Library of Congress Cataloging-in-Publication Data

United States-Japan trade in telecommunications : conflict and
   compromise / edited by Meheroo Jussawalla.
      p.   cm. — (Contributions in economics and economic history,
   ISSN 0084-9235 ; no. 145)
   Includes bibliographical references and index.
   ISBN 0-313-28718-X (alk. paper)
   1. Telecommunication policy—United States. 2. Telecommunication
policy—Japan. 3. Telecommunication equipment industry—Government
policy—United States. 4. Telecommunication equipment industry—
Government policy—Japan. 5. Foreign trade regulation—United
States. 6. Foreign trade regulation—Japan. 7. Foreign trade
promotion—United States. 8. Foreign trade promotion—Japan.
I. Jussawalla, Meheroo. II. Series.
HE7781.U57 1993
384'.068—dc20   92-35597

British Library Cataloguing in Publication Data is available.

Library of Congress Catalog Card Number: 92-35597
ISBN: 0-313-28718-X
ISSN: 0084-9235

First published in 1993

Greenwood Press, 88 Post Road West, Westport, CT 06881
An imprint of Greenwood Publishing Group, Inc.

Printed in the United States of America

The paper used in this book complies with the
Permanent Paper Standard issued by the National
Information Standards Organization (Z39.48–1984).

10 9 8 7 6 5 4 3 2 1

Contents

Preface

The extraordinary dynamism of the Pacific region over the past decade has placed Japan in the lead in setting patterns of telecommunications technology and its usage as integral components of economic development. While the countries of North America and Europe are struggling to emerge from a recession, Japan and the Asian tigers are accumulating trade surpluses in world markets. Japan's gross national product (GNP) has outstripped that of Germany and its per capita GNP is higher than that in the United States. Japan is competing successfully in various industrial goods and in services like banking, trading, and information services. Its share in global trade is growing so rapidly that its prowess constitutes a threat to other economies such as those of Europe and the United States. Even as regionalism in trade is becoming more significant with the formation of the European Single Market and the North American Free Trade Agreement, Japan is growing concerned that the Association of Southeast Asian Nations (ASEAN) countries may also follow the pattern of regional trade blocs, thus isolating the Japanese economy from all three free-trade areas. Underlying these challenges is the future role of Japan in the region. The ASEAN Summit held in 1992 failed to agree on the East Asian Economic Caucus; however, Japan continues to enjoy a trade surplus with both the United States and the ASEAN countries.

The United States, in the past, had held the virtual hegemony in international trade and technological advances. The United States, as the world leader in foreign trade, in foreign direct investment, in innovation, and in technology, was relied on by developing countries for assistance in technology transfer and trade preferences. Today, this hegemony is challenged not only by Japan but by the Asian newly industrialized economies (NIEs).

With these developments in mind, the East-West Center undertook a study of the trade friction in telecommunications between the United States and Japan and the consequent imposition of the Super 301 Clause on Japan. The perception that Japan is an unfair trader has persisted for several decades; thus, although Japan sought General Agreement on Tariffs and Trade (GATT) membership after World War II, it became a member only in 1955. Writing in the *Wall Street Journal* on January 6, 1992, Jagdish Bhagwati shows that even in 1955 40 percent of GATT members invoked Article XXXV of the GATT charter not to extend GATT-defined rights to a new member. Since then, Japan's export surpluses have been countered by demands for voluntary restraints on exports. In the United States over the past five years "Japan bashing" has increased and a protectionist lobby known as the Revisionists has formed.

No precedent in history exists for the current trade conflict between the United States and Japan because the Japanese chose to remain within the orbit of Western influence in their international relations. A great deal of misapprehension and dissension is growing from day to day between the leaders and the people of both nations without concrete changes in market penetration by the United States.

The East-West Center's study focused on the telecommunications sector of the trade between these two economic superpowers. The global market for telecommunications equipment and services in 1990 exceeded $500 billion and is expanding rapidly. This level of activity is leading to global mergers in an effort to secure larger market shares. Balance of payments statistics belie the impact of such mergers on trade. Such mergers circumvent competition and diffuse protectionist trade regulations. For example, Intel Corporation, the largest U.S. semiconductor company, recently announced an alliance with Japanese consumer electronics maker Sharp to develop and manufacture new chips called flash memories. Telecommunications itself is being subjected to policy changes in both countries in an effort to deregulate long-standing monopolies and introduce competition in the domestic and international markets.

Both governments insist that ties remain fundamentally sound. Over the past five years, Japan's trade surplus with the United States has dropped 25 percent to $41 billion in 1990 and U.S. exports to Japan have doubled. The cultural and political differences persist, giving rise to misunderstandings that emerge in trade negotiations. For example, the Japanese system of interlocking directorates of corporations, called the keiretsu, serves to exclude foreign companies from selling their products in Japan. As Japan's investments in the United States grow, returns on these investments will again begin to impact on the trade deficit of the United States. However, as noted in the study undertaken by the East-West Center, the two countries have more to unite them than to divide them. Can the United States learn from the keiretsu to become more competitive? Many U.S. companies with products as diverse as computers, semiconductors, automobiles, and farm implements are revamping their cultures and investment practices to form cooperative links both vertically and horizontally as antitrust policies become more lenient. The horizontal grouping provides security and stability to promote risk taking and investment. Even if pure keiretsu is counter to U.S. policies, U.S. producers need to develop something similar to such an organization.

First and foremost, Japan and the United States account for 40 percent of the world's gross national product. Japan is the world's largest single source of surplus savings and the biggest capital investor. The United States remains the biggest, richest, most productive, and most innovative country. These two countries have had their economies intertwined for several years. One-third of Japanese exports over the past five years have been purchased by the United States. During the same period, Japan has been the largest single investor in the United States. Japan is essential to U.S. trade in the Pacific, and Japan needs U.S. consumer markets. Therefore, trade disputes must be kept in perspective. While it is true that the United States continues to be a melting pot for world cultures — welcoming people from different lands, including the Russians now that the Cold War is over — Japan continues to be isolationist in its immigration policies, and its culture is not universally accepted. Its social organization is uniquely Japanese.

The rapid shift in the two nations' relative economic strength, the chronic trade disputes, and the disappearing threat from the former Soviet Union have affected the military, political, and economic arrangements between the two countries. A global economic partnership is becoming important for peace and security in the Asia-Pacific region. Both Japan and the United States will be major players. Just as Japan needs U.S. markets, the United States depends on Japanese capital to finance both national debt and industrial investment. Both governments have maintained that their relationship is fundamentally sound. It is a misconception to believe that differences in national character create conflict, especially for countries whose national interests are congruent. Both countries want global nuclear balance, stability in Asia, and liberalization of policies in China. Both want to rescue multilateral free trade from the dangers of trading blocs, quotas, and other nontariff barriers. It was the free-trade system that brought Japan its post-war economic miracle. It also permitted the United States to double its manufactured exports from 1986 to 1991. The Japanese-U.S. alliance would be the main pillar of the Pacific Century, and both countries should be attempting to achieve it.

This book begins with a brief report about the research project undertaken by the East-West Center and ends with a chapter on the same study in the perspective of an application of the economic Theory of Games. Domestic telecommunications policies of both Japan and the United States are discussed in detail by Douglas A. Conn in Chapter 2. He emphasizes the impact of these policy differences on trade relations between the two countries. In his chapter we see that Japan undertook divestiture of Nippon Telephone and Telegraph Company (NTT) as a necessary concession for easing the trade conflict and the mounting foreign pressure to open its markets to foreign entrants. But, as Conn points out, treatment of NTT by the Ministry of Posts and Telecommunications has been unbalanced. A case-by-case settlement of trade disputes is not a long-term solution to the conflict, and deregulation in both countries has not helped to reduce the trade imbalance.

The political aspects of the trade dispute are covered by Fumiko Mori Halloran in Chapter 3. She shows how the trade issues have real political causes that surface when, during negotiations such as the Structural Impediments Initiative, the Japanese attempt to tell the U.S. representatives how to run their country and the Americans tell the Japanese how to run their businesses. In her opinion there is a political confrontation in which trade is used as a tool by both countries.

Japan's trade in telecommunications services is exhaustively covered by Hajime Oniki (Chapter 4), who has provided a wealth of data on the trade in semiconductors by using price deflators and foreign exchange rates to show the trade imbalance. Telecommunications services are based on software in which Japan does not have a comparative advantage. Japan is one of three countries that permits free resale of leased circuits and, therefore, is liberal in its telecommunications business. However, he indicates that many barriers to foreign entrants still remain.

In Chapter 5, Jonathan Aronson describes the international climate for telecommunications trade and deals comprehensively with the U.S. Telecommunications Annex in its attempt to identify the rules of the game. His chapter traces the history of the emergence of services in the Uruguay Round of the GATT trade talks and the difficulties faced by the negotiating parties in regard to this important issue.

Industrial countries had agreed to have a telecommunications annex, and even Japan was supportive of the U.S. position at GATT. Against this background Shinzo Kobori (Chapter 6) presents the perspective of the Japanese private sector on the trade talks at GATT with reference to telecommunications services. He discusses the distribution system in Japan as well as Japan's antitrust policy and how these factors impact on the trade imbalance between Japan and the United States.

The GATT theme is continued by Marcellus S. Snow (Chapter 7), who examines the role of international organiza-tions in the expansion of trade in services. The ASEAN countries have an important contribution to make to telecommunications trade between the United States and Japan, and to that extent a case study of the region's trade is the focus of this chapter.

The cultural aspects of the trade disputes between Japan and the United States have emerged as a significant factor in negotiations, and these aspects are examined in detail by Joseph Doherty (Chapter 8). His scrutiny of cultural differences illustrates some of the seemingly irreconcilable differences between the leaders and corporate executives of both countries.

Chapter 9 attempts to apply the economic Theory of Games to the trade imbalance in specific information technologies, which helps to advance the analysis in concrete terms. It recommends changes in the friction cycle to establish "a level playing field" for trade between the two countries.

The economic and sociopolitical implications of this work were highlighted when the U.S. president undertook a special visit to Japan January 7–10, 1992, in an effort to "open Japanese markets to American exports." Whether Japan is efficient or exclusionist in its trade policy can be understood if we look at the import data for 1990. In that year Japan was the world's third largest importer, buying $52 billion worth of goods (*The Economist*, January 11, 1992). However, Japan exported $52 billion more than it imported. As a proportion of gross domestic product, Japan and the United States import 8 percent and 10 percent, respectively, compared with 23 percent by Germany. In industrial products, tariff and non-tariff barriers average similarly in the Organization for Economic Cooperation and Development countries with 2.6 percent in Japan, 3 percent in the United States, and 2.9 percent in the European Community. The imports in Japan are clustered according to the principle of comparative advantage, as seen in the table.

Japan's Trade in 1990, by Category
(in billions of dollars)

	Exports	Imports
Foodstuffs	1.6	31.6
Raw materials	1.9	28.5
Fuels	1.3	56.7
Chemicals	15.9	16.0
Motor vehicles	51.0	6.4
Machinery and transport equipment	150.3	31.5
Other manufactures	60.3	57.9
Miscellaneous	4.6	6.2

Source: Japanese Ministry of Finance.

The concept that Japan follows adversarial trade practices cannot be supported fully by such data. The truth in telecommunications trade seems to be that Japanese businesses are protectionist when it suits their interests, as shown in Chapter 9 of this book. When developing a new product or nurturing sales of an existing one, Japanese businesses get their market protected against competition because of their closeness to the Ministry of International Trade and Industry. The U.S. managed-trade approach does not seem to offer a lasting solution to the deficit with Japan. The characteristic of international trade is to allow the two trading countries to specialize. Trade barriers are not the most efficient form of achieving the most mutually beneficial results. Markets and relative prices will achieve this result anyway. Dividing the market between semiconductor makers or manufacturers of cellular telephones thwarts the process of specialization through trade. The goal of the Uruguay Round is just this: to devise trade rules that will allow specialization to achieve welfare for trading partners. Protectionist trends need to be curbed at all levels of policy for global markets to flourish and impart prosperity multilaterally.

The new world order as envisaged by President Bush would require a rapprochement between the United States and Japan on the basis of a cultural understanding between the two nations. Strong leadership of both of these countries is essential for the stability and development of the entire Asia-Pacific region and, ultimately, for global prosperity as well. Although market economies operate in both countries, they do so in different ways, and these differences need to be accepted. Corporate values and techniques differ, which leads to different results, but this difference does not indicate inefficiency on the part of any single system. It is not just the quantity of the trade deficit that is causing misunderstanding between the two trading partners but the composition of that deficit as well. The assumptions behind trade in telecommunications equipment, as we have seen, are of perfect competition and constant returns to scale. Technological innovations and investments in research and development are also factors to be reckoned with in any analysis of trade relations. The mentor role of the United States in its trade policy does not permit a better understanding of why Japan sells it semiconductors below cost in the United States. Consumers play a more dominant role in the United States on the basis of individualism, whereas in Japan production based on group intensive factors make the keiretsu thrive. Pragmatic arrangements have to be worked out between countries in order to account for structural and historical differences. The differences have to be recognized to provide a strong economic foundation for a stable United States-Japan partnership. The three largest markets globally are in Japan, the United States, and Europe. U.S. firms have eliminated the deficit with Europe and sell their products comfortably within the domestic market, but the dominance of the large keiretsu prevents them from selling in Japanese markets. Therefore, many U.S. suppliers of telecommunications equipment are forming alliances with their Japanese counterparts to capture a share in their market (see Chapter 1). An example of the United States' aim to remain competitive in the global market is found in the super-computer industry. The United States has blocked dumping in the U.S. market and has demanded sales in Japan. A perception gap between the two countries that needs to be rectified persists. While Japan has become one of the world's largest donor countries, it still has to transcend narrow self-interest and rise to its international role as an economic, financial, and technological superpower. A reduction in trade friction is only part of this responsibility. The major change will come when the Japanese economy is transformed from being totally export driven to being demand driven. Shared interest in democracy and economic welfare will bring benefits to both societies.

UNITED STATES-JAPAN TRADE IN TELECOMMUNICATIONS

Introduction

Meheroo Jussawalla

The United States and Japan are the world's largest and second largest democracies. Both have an interest in shaping international trade policies, and both are aware of the important role of communications in rendering such policies effective. Since the industrial rehabilitation of Japan in the 1950s, both Japan and the United States have enjoyed a mutually beneficial economic relationship. For the fiscal year ending March 31, 1991, Japan recorded a trade surplus of $88.35 billion, the second highest total on record. Its exports rose by 8.1 percent, and imports declined by 4.2 percent, the first drop in five years. Even with a faltering domestic economy, Japanese companies are aggressively shipping excess production overseas. But these data also underscore the danger that a weakened Japanese economy will reduce opportunities for U.S. companies to increase their exports to Japan, especially when the recession in the United States is reducing overall growth.

The global system has become increasingly interdependent, and world trade has grown from $2.9 trillion in 1980 to approximately $4 trillion in 1991. The share of U.S. exports during that period is declining. Japan's exports as a ratio of gross national product have risen from 12.6 percent in 1979 to 14 percent in 1990.

Many reasons exist for the strained relations in trade between Japan and the United States and for the current Japan bashing prevalent at even the highest levels. One reason is that the role of information as an incentive to trade relations is neglected. International transmission of information influences changes in elasticity of demand for goods and services in both consumer and capital markets. The degree of change is dependent on the quality and reliability of the information transmitted across national borders.

The economics literature has developed a powerful case against markets as guarantors of efficiency even if there is free competition in traded goods (Helleiner 1978). International markets are creatures of political and social systems, which makes communications one of the most powerful sources exercising leverage in international trade relationships. This role of information intensity in assessing the terms of trade has been neglected in the existing international economic order, hence the need for the General Agreement on Tariffs and Trade (GATT) in the Uruguay Round of trade talks to include a charter on trade in services with a special focus on telecommunications services.

Transnational corporations (TNCs) transmit and exchange large quantities of information intrafirm rather than through market channels. They have set up their own private data and voice networks that bypass the common carriers and yield economies in costs. For such TNCs, information is traded like a durable capital good because it results in a stream of future benefits. In an oligopolistic market situation, Magdoff (1976) claims that the power of generating information is so great with TNCs that international trade is no longer the sole vehicle for the international exchange of goods and services. The United Nations Center for Transnational Corporations has done several studies on trade in services under the supervision of Karl Sauvant. The most recent study deals with service industries, government policies, and trade relationships in a survey of the Uruguay Round (Messerlin, Sauvant, & Belassa 1990).

The role of information flows in promoting trade opportunities is better recognized in Japan than in the United States. For example, Japan budgets $48 million a year for its external trade organization and the Japanese External Trade Organization takes care of the export ventures in the country. The question is frequently raised as to why Japan is winning the trade war, not only with the United States but with Europe and Asia as well. This success is not wholly attributable to illegal trade practices such as the dumping of products at below production costs. Most Japanese business cycles, including the current downturn, are tackled by government intervention rather than by boosting exports. Undoubtedly exports are crucial to Japan because imports are indispensable. But the perceived need after the oil crisis of the 1970s has been to export or perish. Therefore, they have mastered the dynamics of international trade and have devised an export strategy based on the accumulation of production experience. Therefore, the relationship of cost to volume is calculated, and unit costs decline at a constant rate each time production experience doubles. The rate of decline depends on the type of product, for example, for TV sets it is 15 percent and for automobiles it is 12 percent.

Generally Japanese firms forfeit short-term profits in order to grow more rapidly and to increase their market share. This weakens the position of rival firms. The principles of production economics are not as widely applied in the United States because the domestic market is more mature than the Japanese market, and long-term decline in unit costs in the United States is overtaken by inflation. After World War II, Japan started at the low end of the technology spectrum with transistor radios and tape recorders and posed no threat to U.S. producers. By the 1960s, the Japanese became the most cost-efficient producers of consumer electronics. The output of Japanese color television sets tripled every year after 1966, and unit costs fell by 40 percent each year compared with U.S. production, where costs for the same product fell by only 6 percent annually. The Japanese also have an accurate sense of timing their export campaigns. They enter a market when elasticity of demand is declining, that is, when demand is becoming stable irrespective of price changes. The Japanese then shift gears when elasticity changes. In contrast, U.S. producers shifted their semiconductor production to Korea, Hong Kong, and Taiwan in order to compete with the Japanese. This engendered technology transfer to the Asian countries who soon became rivals in international markets.

These developments led to several analyses of the trade friction between Japan and the United States, both before and after the imposition of the 301 Clause by the U.S. trade representative (USTR) in 1989. U.S. resurgence in the age of the pacific was discussed in a book entitled *The Third Century*, by Joel Kotkin and Yoriko Kishimoto (1988). This book deals with the shift of the world's economic center of gravity to the pacific and shows how the United States can and should play a pivotal role in the shaping of future events in the region. It is well-documented with statistical data and relates success stories of Asian Americans and their contribution to the U.S. economy. Also analyzed are the market opportunities that will be created in Taiwan, Singapore, Korea, and China for U.S. exports as well as for collaborative ventures. The book explodes the myth of Japanese invincibility and emphasizes the trend of Japanese investments in the United States as stemming from the long-term strength of the U.S. economy. In fact, the book reiterates the advantages of the open economy in the United States, which permit it to function as a world nation.

The misconceptions that cloud the understanding of the Japanese miracle are removed in Bill Emmott's book *The Sun Also Sets* (1989). He predicted that Japan was enjoying a temporary period of financial and economic superiority to which there are limitations. This book supports the thesis of *The Third Century* and convincingly explains why Japan's growing capital surplus does not make it an economic superpower that can ride out cyclical changes. This thesis has been proved by the 1992 declines in the Japanese stock market and the lower growth rate for the coming year. Emmott argues that Japan will not be able to take over from the United States as the leading power in a nonpolar world without a sizable military and a stronger role in international affairs.

Another publication that deals with Japanese trade surplus is written by the academic defender of multilateral trade, Jagdish Bhagwati who, in a book entitled *The World Trading System at Risk* (1990), sets at rest the fear that the United States is a diminished giant. The book traces the history of United States-Japan trade since the 1930s and shows how Voluntary Export Restraints have been operating for Japan for over five decades. Japan grew too quickly for its competitors, who have generally settled their trade disputes by bilateral agreements. *The Economist* (June 1, 1991) predicted that by 1993 the United States will have eliminated its trade deficit with Japan on the basis that Japan's imports have doubled in dollars since 1986 and that the U.S. deficit in 1991 was less than half of what it was in 1986. Clyde Prestowitz, in his work *Trading Places: How We Allowed Japan to Take the Lead* (1989), dealt with the same issue of United States-Japan trade and cautioned U.S. policymakers of overreacting to the Japanese trade surplus.

A critical study of Japanese society as it actually works was authored by Karel van Wolferen (1989) who lived and worked in Japan for 20 years. He shows how Japan's economic prowess has created great apprehension among its trading partners in Europe and the United States because it is not playing an adequate part in international relations and is not global in its outreach. He carefully delves into Japanese politics to show that Japan does not have a responsible central government. He also examines Japan's indus-trial system to declare that the Japanese economy is not a fully free-market economy and that many of its industrial policies are dictated by the government.

According to Lester Thurow in his new book *Head to Head: The Coming Economic Battles among Japan, Europe and America*, the age of specialization in trade is over and that in the twenty-first century there will be head-to-head competition. All three powers want the same key industries, which means that some will win and others will lose, unlike the earlier niche markets. It has been widely assumed in the United States and Europe that Japan is the source of all trading tensions caused by its protectionist policies. According to this analysis, it is Europe and not Japan that initiated the policy for managed trade. In March 1992, the USTR's office published its annual report on trade barriers abroad. This report states that Europe is considered more of a threat to free trade than Japan. Thurow predicts that because Europe will be the largest trading block the world has ever known, other countries should also form trade blocks. However, regional free trade areas are not a good substitute for multilateral free trade. Already the North American Free Trade Agreement is causing concerns in the Asia-Pacific region and led to the Malaysian proposal for an East Asian economic caucus. This proposal was not favorably viewed by other Association of Southeast Asian Nations countries at the Singapore Summit in early 1992.

Bhagwati and Patrick (1992), in their recent work entitled *Aggressive Unilateralism*, which examines the United States' 1988 Omnibus Trade Act with special reference to the 301 and Super 301 clauses and their enforcement, claim that, in recent years, U.S. trade policy has moved toward unilateralism. In this book, Makoto Kuroda argues that the imposition of Super 301 on Japan has clearly damaged the relationship between the two countries and that it is especially damaging to the multilateralism supported by the GATT. He suggests that there is a misconception of economic realities and that the trade deficit faced by the United States should be tackled by other methods. Exchange rate adjustment had failed to give the necessary impetus to U.S. exports, which led to the belief that access to Japanese markets was to blame. The macroeconomic roots of this problem lie in controlling U.S. government spending and boosting domestic savings.

As the services sectors of both countries increase in importance, GATT's role in devising a new services charter also becomes crucial. This is especially true of telecommunications services that have been one of the irritants in the United States-Japan trade dispute. Japan's services sector now accounts for 63 percent of GNP compared with 57 percent in Germany, 63 percent in the United Kingdom, and 71 percent in the United States. The telecommunications sector alone is funneling $79 billion a year into Japan's total output. Unilateral protectionism on the part of the United States will only lead to further deterioration in trade relations between the two countries. Michael Porter's (1990) thesis in his book *The Competitive Advantage of Nations* is relevant to this conflict as he argues for competition rather than comparative advantage for trade to be successful. In either case, free trade would be a required assumption. Porter uses the input-output methodology to measure social income accounts and from them he measures forward and backward linkages to establish investments in different industries. Increasing demand from U.S. industries for sophisticated telecommunications equipment was met by Japanese suppliers at competitive prices and even the U.S. defense program's demand was met similarly.

Tension between the United States and Japan grew when Japan bashing became fashionable among U.S. intelligentsia and was responded to by similar rebuffs from Japanese leaders. One such inflammatory work was published in 1989 by Shintaro Ishihara and Akio Morita (1989) called *The Japan That Can Say No* in which the authors challenge U.S. domestic policies and claim that Japan can do just as well without U.S. trade relations. This book was translated and widely disclaimed in Japan itself. In fact, Morita later disassociated himself from the previous work by publishing an article on why Japan must change and trade by global rules. This was translated and published in *Fortune* (March 9, 1992) under the title "Why Japan Must Change." He was critical of Japan's price-fixing policies and its corporate behavior. The stockholders of Japanese companies played a passive role compared with their U.S. counterparts and needed to change. If Japan is to survive in a global economy it must learn to accept the fact that it is part of a borderless world. A book of that title, authored by Kenichi Ohmae (1990) became the center of attention in corporate circles around the globe. He advanced the thesis that corporations need to tailor their output according to global demands because political boundaries are fast disappearing and corporate policies should cater to the demands of international consumers rather than to country-specific demands.

An invaluable framework for both policymakers and practitioners was written by Jonathan Aronson and Peter Cowhey and published as *When Countries Talk; International Trade in Telecommunications Services.* The authors explore the industries that are reshaping the rules for international trade in services and show a strong link between equipment trade and services trade in the telecommunications sector. In this volume, Aronson examines the recent developments in GATT and the pros and cons of the Telecoms Annex. In an article published in *The Wall Street Journal* (April 21, 1992), Karen Elliot House declares that the Japanese are not the terminators of the U.S. economy, as is widely believed, because they are vulnerable to the same market forces that shape the economies of other countries. In the last quarter of 1991, the Japanese economy contracted and the first quarter of 1992 shows no growth. In March 1992, Japan's stock market experienced a precipitous fall, and since 1989 the Tokyo market has fallen by more than half. The Japanese still view their economy as sound but not invincible. The downturn signals the close of a period when Japan's money culture leaped ahead of its real growth. By 1990 Japan's overall private investment had reached 30 percent of its gross domestic product (GDP), roughly double that of the United States. Now that money is no longer cheap in Japan, changes are under way within firms and financial markets. *Business Week* (April 27, 1991) queries if Japan will lose its competitive edge. The stock market crash wiped out $2.6 trillion in value on the Tokyo Stock Exchange. This is likely to erode Japan's global edge, but Japanese companies in the past have surmounted such setbacks with fierce competition and may do the same this time. Japan's most impressive success has been in microelectronics, and Sony has its plant just outside Nagoya. Hitachi's research center is focused on developing chips that can store 1 billion bits of data as compared with 4 million stored on chips today. Such advances guarantee that the world's consumer electronics makers will become increasingly reliant on Japanese supplies. Corporations like Intel announced in February 1992 that Japan's Sharp Corporation will serve as its strategic partner in flash memory chips.

Japan is now trying to export its way out of a recession. The keiretsus are moving toward erosion of cross-shareholding. Any further weakening of the keiretus could prevent its members from taking risks and will introduce greater convergence between U.S. and Japanese business practices. Weaker electronic firms will face takeovers, but investment in research and development will be diluted because of the higher costs of financing it. The Ministry of International Trade and Industry is offering research and development subsidies and pressing business firms to move into new avenues that have greater profit potential. Even a company like Matsushita Electric Industrial Company, which is a giant in factory automation, is grappling with the aftershocks of the stock market crash. In the past, low interest rates and cheap equity capital had fueled an investment surge that is rapidly losing steam. Japan cannot run a $1 trillion current account surplus without incurring huge problems.

With all the difficulties facing the Japanese economy caused by the fluctuations in the stock market and the slowing economy, there is a relentless drive for improvement that runs through Japanese corporate culture.

America's personal computer companies will seek their components from Japan despite the recession. Sometimes it is envisaged as unfair competition, and some Japanese agree that a change in their practices is needed. The Kedanrin is strong in its support of Japanese ascendancy in the export market and the maintenance of Deming-type quality control on exports. France's former prime minister, Edith Cresson, made charges that Japan had "an overwhelming desire to conquer the world." Morita agrees that Japanese firms should change their mission of victory in the marketplace for a more tolerant view of competitors.

Efforts are being made to ease the global views about Japan's mercantilism by marginal changes in Japanese policies and by the types of view expressed by Kenichi Ohmae (1990). This view was voiced in 1990 in an article entitled "Who is US?" published in the *Harvard Business Review* by Robert Reich, who maintains that U.S. corporations often produce outside and foreign corporations produce in the United States. He concludes that U.S. competitiveness can be best defined as the capacity of the country to add value to the world economy regardless of the nationality of the company. In "Who is US?" Reich asks "Is it IBM, Motorola, Whirlpool, and General

Motors? Or is it Sony, Thomson, Philips, and Honda?" The question then is how do we define national interest in a newly globalized economy? The prosperity of each country will ultimately depend on the skills of its workers and managers rather than the flag of its corporations. To that end, we need a more realistic policy on trade, technology transfer, and market access.

As far back as 1978, President Carter had turned in a report to Congress on Export Promotion Functions. Congress than passed the Trade Agreements Act of 1979 to improve U.S. export performance and to participate more fully in multilateral trade negotiations. Since then Japan has endeavored to meet deadlines imposed on it by U.S. trade negotiators. In 1981 Japan agreed to liberalize its procurement policies of Nippon Telephone and Telegraph Company to enable U.S. exporters to bid for orders. In December of 1981, Japan eased its restrictions on data entering the country. It is now committed to tariffs not exceeding 3.2 percent on all GATT-negotiated industrial products. Even so, Japan does not favor a sizable inflow of foreign capital. Foreign-owned equity in Japan constitutes only 4 percent of total manufactures. It has consistently discouraged foreign-owned subsidiaries. The United States-Japan trade account cannot be balanced on a bilateral basis. Even an appreciated yen does not take too large a toll of Japanese exports. For example, in March 1992 Japanese merchandise trade surplus jumped 29.3 percent to $10.99 billion (*Wall Street Journal*, April 14, 1992), which increases the concern that, with Japan's domestic economy slowing down, Japanese companies will ship excess production overseas. It also underscores the danger that a weakened Japanese economy will reduce opportunities for U.S. exports to that country.

The impasse on how each country should promote its exports and at what speed poses repercussions on the global market. So long as Japan arbitrarily restricts its overall economic growth rate little room exists for increasing its imports. Studies by the Organization for Economic Cooperation and Development (OECD) show that Japan must achieve a real growth rate of more than 6 percent to expand imports. In the early 1980s it appeared as if the appreciating yen might yield the benefits of the J Curve to the United States because Japanese imports were mounting. But the tight money policy in Japan brought about capital outflow from Japan, diluting the effect of what might have been the benefits of the J Curve.

During his visit to Japan in early 1992, President Bush requested that Japan open its markets to imports. When we look at the table of the world's 10 top importers, we find that in 1990 Japan was the world's third largest importer, having bought $235 billion worth of goods from abroad. Even so in that year it had a surplus of $52 billion.

World's Top 10 Importers

1990	Value $ Bn	% Share of World Imports	Imports per Head $
United States	517	14.3	2,050
Germany	356	9.9	4,460
Japan	235	6.5	1,900
France	234	6.5	4,150
Britain	223	6.2	3,890
Italy	182	5.0	3,160
Holland	126	3.5	8,460
Canada	124	3.4	4,660
USSR	121	3.3	4,180
Belgium-Lux	120	3.3	11,540

Source: GATT, OECD, *The Economist* (January 11, 1992).

As a proportion of GDP, both Japan and the United States score low compared with Europe. The main question that baffles policymakers in the United States is do price signals operate in Japan? Even if we look at average tariffs, we find that Japan's tariff on industrial products is 2.6 percent compared with 3 percent in the United States. According to the *Brookings Papers* 1991 (Volume 1), the non-tariff barriers have risen equally in both countries and Japan's propensity to import depends on other factors such as culture, industrial structure, and bureaucratic discretion. Robert Lawrence in the above-cited *Brookings Papers* deals with the industrial structure and the close-knit industrial groups as restricting imports. The difficulty lies in measuring the amount of restriction that keiretsus impose on imports. Does their activity really interfere with comparative advantage?

The new markets that are emerging are not consumer goods or producer goods markets according to Peter Drucker in an article entitled "Where the New Markets Are" in the *Wall Street Journal* (April 9, 1992). The most immediate and accessible of the new markets cluster around communication and information. This is the market that both the United States and Japan are trying to capture.

In the so-called managed trade game, countries agree to share markets, but this will not add to their competitive strength. In an article entitled, "A Dangerous Fix for Trade Deficits" in *Fortune* (May 4, 1992), Lee Smith contends that managed trade is only a respectable garment for protectionism. Such managed trade agreements have cost U.S. consumers $60–$70 billion annually over the past decade. Yet, in the same article Clyde Prestowitz points out that without managed trade, the U.S. semiconductor industry would be wiped out. Thus, a semiconductor agreement between the United States and

Japan was signed in 1986 even though the terms have not been fully implemented. Managed trade actually erodes the benefits of free trade, discourages new entrants, and hinders innovation in the long term. Despite these agreements, Japan's semiconductor firms are being left behind in a race to master the next generation devices. U.S. chip makers, led by Intel, have won more than 90 percent of the burgeoning market for flash memories. The irony is that flash memories are a Japanese invention. Although the Semiconductor Agreement was renewed in July 1991, the Japanese have so far not dumped their chips with flash memory on world markets at below costs.

In summary, the competition and reproachment of the United States and Japan is headed toward the new cultural world order. *The Economist* has rightly pointed out in an article entitled "Forget Pearl Harbor" (November 30, 1991), that the United States will never be Europe and Japan will never be Asia. Japan is the only country in Asia that has adopted European culture. Despite their trade differences, both the United States and Japan will achieve their economic synthesis in the near future. For the United States, despite its identity crisis, this is a remarkable time in history. As the world order is changing, the competition between nations is no longer for geopolitical power but for standard of living: the ability of a country to provide its citizens with security, comfort, and progress. While the economist, Paul Krugman, foresaw *The Age of Diminished Expectations* (1990), the future for the United States in a nonpolar world is one for optimism.

REFERENCES

Aronson, Jonathan and Peter Cowhey. 1988. *When Countries Talk: International Trade in Telecommunications Services.* Cambridge, MA: Ballinger Publishing.

Bhagwati, Jagdish. 1991. *The World Trading System at Risk.* New York: Harvester Wheatsheaf.

Bhagwati, Jagdish and Hugh Patrick. 1992. *Aggressive Unilateralism.* Ann Arbor: University of Michigan Press.

Emmott, Bill. 1989. *The Sun Also Sets.* New York: Random House.

Helleiner, G. 1978. "World Market Imperfections and Developing Countries." Occasional Papers II Overseas, Development Council. Washington, DC.

Ishihara, Shintaro and Akio Morita. 1989. *The Japan That Can Say No.* English Translation Mimeo. Washington, DC.

Kotkin, Joel and Yoriko Kishimoto. 1988. *The Third Century.* New York: Crown Publishers.

Krugman, Paul. 1990. *The Age of Diminished Expectations.* Cambridge, MA: MIT Press.

Magdoff, Harry. 1976. "Multinational Corporations and Social Development." In *Multinational Corporations,* edited by David Apter and Louis Wolf Goodman, Chapter 8. New York: Praeger.

Messerlin, Patrick, Karl Sauvant, and Bela Belassa. 1990. *The Uruguay Round: Services in the World Economy*. Washington, DC: World Bank and United Nations Center for Transnational Corporations.

Ohmae, Kenichi. 1990. *The Borderless World*. New York: Harper Business.

Porter, Michael. 1990. *The Competitive Advantage of Nations*. New York: Free Press.

Prestowitz, Clyde. 1989. *Trading Places: How We Allowed Japan to Take the Lead*. New York: Basic Books.

Thurow, Lester. 1992. *Head to Head: The Coming Economic Battles among Japan, Europe, and America*. New York: William Morrow.

van Wolferen, Karel. 1989. *The Enigma of Japanese Power*. New York: Knopf.

1

Telecommunications Trade Friction: The United States and Japan

Meheroo Jussawalla and Barbara Ross-Pfeiffer

Because of a trade imbalance, friction has recently been steadily increasing between the United States and Japan. While some believe that macroeconomic factors are the cause of this imbalance, many in Congress and others from the U.S. business community blame unfair trade practices by their Japanese competitors. Negative popular sentiment toward the other country is increasing in both countries, as nationalistic pressures in both countries become stronger. Yet, historically speaking, no precedent for the current United States-Japan conflict exists, as Japan has always remained in the orbit of the western world regarding international relations. The greatest challenge for the leaders of both countries is to combine their strengths in economic terms and in the pursuit of democratic values.

During the past four decades the world has turned into a multipolar system. Emerging nations in the vibrant Pacific region have become increasingly important in the international trading system, a system that depends on the reliable flow of information. Foremost among the emerging nations of the Pacific, Japan plays a prominent role in setting the patterns of telecommunications usage and in the introduction of intelligent communications systems. Therefore, Japan is threatening the economic and technical superiority of the United States and challenging the virtual hegemony that the United States has occupied in the international economy and the global trading system. Four decades ago, the United States was not only the world's manufacturing and agricultural center but also dominated innovation, science, and technology. Now, with its gross national product (GNP) reaching $4 trillion, Japan is home to eight of the world's ten largest public companies and boasts seven of the world's largest banks. Emmott (1989) points out that high savings and skillful approaches to production, trade, and finance have permitted Japan to achieve impressive economic success. However, the U.S. savings-investment gap is being filled by the rest of the world. Adding to Japan's economic influence is the fast pace of development of Asia's newly industrialized economies. These countries are emulating Japan by creating non-tariff barriers against imports of telecommunications equipment on the plea of incompatibility of standards.

The Association of Southeast Asian Nations (ASEAN) and the countries of the Pacific Rim constitute a critical marketplace in the trade future of both Japan and the United States. With Japan as the ASEAN countries' largest trading partner and the United States as their second largest (Figure 1.1), this new dynamic element emerging in the Pacific region is causing competition between the United States and Japan to intensify as both countries attempt to gain a greater share of this critical market and to expand their share of the global market. The global market for telecommunications equipment and services exceeded $400 billion in 1989. Deregulation and strict rules against expansion of the regional Bell operating companies has impeded the global reach of the U.S. industry.

FIGURE 1.1
Trade and the Pacific Rim Nations
(in US$ billion)

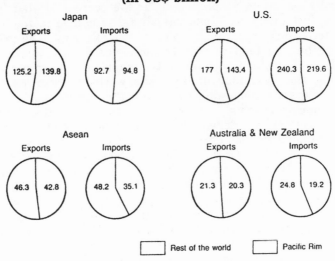

Source: International Monetary Fund.

Japan's trade surplus declined by 17 percent in 1989. This figure may be misleading as Japan's oil imports increased, weakening the yen. As a result, the surplus was calculated at ¥122 per dollar instead of ¥145 per dollar, which was the rate used in 1988. This change may have led to a misinterpretation of the data.

The telecommunications component of this surplus largely results from Japanese exports of semiconductors to the United States. Despite the bilateral agreement on semiconductors negotiated in 1986, the United States still supplies less than 10 percent of the Japanese chip market. Friction generated over semiconductors has been so pervasive that it is known as the chip wars. Other bilateral agreements, such as the 1985 Market Oriented Sector Specific agreements on telecommunications, appear to have had little effect in reducing the telecommunications component of the surplus (Jussawalla 1987).

Most of the trade problems between the United States and Japan have been addressed outside the purview of the General Agreement on Tariffs and Trade (GATT) through bilateral agreements. When a trade dispute is solved through a bilateral agreement, GATT, which is devoted to promoting freer trade through multilateral negotiations, does not have any binding authority. Yet Japan and the United States turn to GATT to keep each other's markets open.

To avoid trade friction, and as part of a new strategy for globalization, mergers and joint ventures are emerging as a means of entry into new markets. Global mergers circumvent competition and diffuse protectionist trade measures.

This chapter will first examine the background of trade theory and non-tariff barriers that impinge on the telecommunications trade. The impact of mergers within the telecommunications sector will also be covered in the first section. Next, we will examine the race for technical superiority between the two countries in telecommunications, semiconductors, computers, and satellites, and then the current Uruguay Round of trade talks being held at GATT will be the focus. Finally, this chapter analyzes trade relations between the United States and Japan, which leads to the conclusion that free trade policies in telecommunications are the most appropriate.

TRADE ISSUES IN TELECOMMUNICATIONS AND THE IMPACT OF MERGERS

A significant part of the telecommunications trade is in the services sector, and telecommunications services are a vital portion of total international trade in services, which is valued at $1 trillion. The flows of data that accompany trade are as important as services because they deal with information about markets, commercial information, product description, technical data, and information about the general framework of trade and monetary policies of the trading partners (Jussawalla, Snow, and Braunstein 1988).

Because goods and services related to information are among the most dynamic sectors of the trade between Japan and the United States, restrictions naturally cause friction and adversely affect trade relations. A survey of tariff and non-tariff measures showed, however, that, with the exception of agriculture, Japan has few formal non-tariff measures (Kreinin 1988). Therefore, the practices that U.S. manufacturers complain about tend to be related to consumer and business practices. Japan has consistently denied that its markets are closed and blames, among other things, the inability of U.S. manufacturers to produce the kinds of goods that are desired by Japanese consumers and producers.

Traditional trade theory, based on comparative advantage, has failed to explain both the current trade friction and the patterns of trade between the two countries. Traditional trade theory did not attempt to explain trade in services because services were considered as intermediate rather than final output. Thus, the role of services in international trade has been inadequately explored, and the quantification of the services sector, its productivity, and its pricing systems are only vaguely understood. Developments in telecommunications technology have challenged the conventional concept, and information services are now traded as final goods.

On September 4, 1989, after some preliminary discussions, an unprecedented round of trade talks dubbed the Structural Impediments Initiative (SII) began in Tokyo. The SII was aimed at addressing the root causes of the trade imbalance, which remained at $50 billion. On April 4, 1990, after the fourth round of SII, the United States and Japan reached an interim agreement. The proposal submitted to both governments included, among other things, deregulation of Japan's complex distribution system and increased enforcement of antitrust laws. The United States responded to Japan's call for specific changes in U.S. economic policies, including reducing the budget deficit and increasing savings and investment.

In early April 1990, the two countries faced deadlines on at least 12 other trade agreements. Japan had been named as a priority country, under the Super 301 clause of the U.S. Omnibus Trade and Competitiveness Act on May 25, 1989, for exclusionary government procurement for satellites and supercomputers and restrictive standards for wood products. Under the trade act, the U.S. trade representative (USTR) is also required to review annually all bilateral telecommunications agreements. Semiconductors, supercomputers, and satellites have become crucial components of the trade conflict between the countries.

The mounting political anxiety over trade relations with Japan was threatening to restrict U.S. flexibility in dealing with the GATT round of trade talks. Simultaneously, demands for protectionist measures were mounting in the United States. In response, Japan unveiled its Buy American plan for 1990. The Ministry of International Trade and Industry (MITI) launched a round of initiatives aimed at speeding imports of manufactures from the United States by at least 10 percent. Such efforts include the earmarking of $1.5 billion in loans to importers and $1.5 billion for a data bank that will link foreign exporters with Japanese importers (Feldstein 1990). However, former Prime Minister Nakasone's Import Now Program and other programs of a similar nature were not effective. Japan's largest export promotion plan may help to reduce the trade gap depending on the response from Japanese companies.

Although the SII talks, other bilateral agreements, and the GATT should significantly reduce the trade friction, Japan's growing share of the trade deficit will probably not decline significantly in the near future (Figure 1.2). The United States has eliminated its trade deficit with Europe and reduced it with other countries. The Japanese surplus therefore continues to confound the U.S. Congress as trade with Japan accounts for 40 percent of the U.S. trade deficit. The continuing surplus also generates criticism from revisionists in the United States. The revisionists hold that a self-oriented Japan is incapable of implementing free market changes without external pressure from its trading partners.

All the above measures, however, cannot compensate for the shortcomings of U.S. macroeconomic policies. The International Monetary Fund in its *World Economic Outlook* for 1990 called attention to the macroeconomic imbalances in the U.S. economy and suggested that any attempts to deal with these imbalances through trade policies would be ineffective. Japanese negotiators at the SII talks expressed concern over the low savings rate in the United States, while as far back as 1985 U.S. trade policy set a goal of reducing Japan's savings in the U.S. at 6.6 percent compared with the average Japanese household, which saved 15.1 percent of its income in the same year (Figure 1.3). Japan abolished the "maruyu" tax-free status of savings on the recommendation of the Maekawa Commission in 1987 in an effort to reduce incentives for savings and thus lower the savings rate. However, neither did the trade friction end nor was the trade gap reduced. The new Japanese plans must therefore change either the rate of savings or total Japanese investment, otherwise the trade surplus will remain unchanged. This fact applies to the trade surplus that Japan has not only with the United States but also with its other trading partners. At present, Japan controls one-tenth of the world's total trade.

The underlying causes of the trade friction that Japan continues to encounter with the United States and the European Economic Community (EEC) are complex, but they mostly amount to an

FIGURE 1.2
1991 Computer Sales by Sector

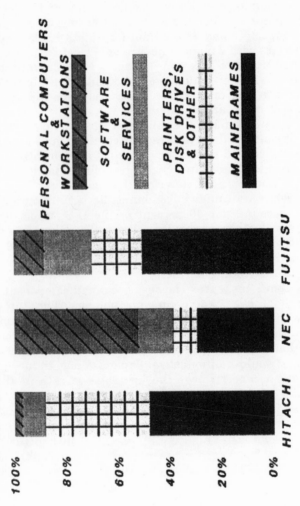

Source: Japan Dataquest, January 1991.

FIGURE 1.3
U.S. Trade Surplus/Deficit with Japan and the European Community
(in US$ billion)

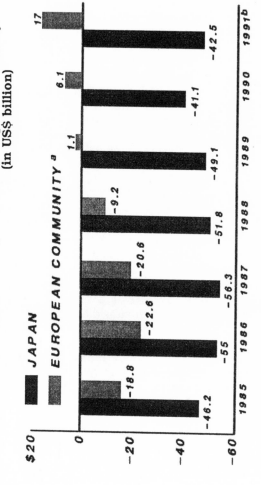

■ JAPAN

▨ EUROPEAN COMMUNITY ᵃ

	1985	1986	1987	1988	1989	1990	1991ᵇ

$20
0
-20
-40
-60

-46.2 -18.8
-55 -22.6
-56.3 -20.6
-51.8 -9.2
-49.1 1.1
-41.1 6.1
-42.5 17

ᵃThe 12 countries in the European Community are Italy, France, Great Britain, Portugal, Spain, Belgium, The Netherlands, Germany, Luxembourg, Greece, Denmark, and Ireland.

ᵇFigures for 1991 are estimated

Source: U.S. Department of Commerce.

19

unwillingness on the part of western suppliers to treat Japan on a par with other well-established suppliers in the global marketplace (Wilson, 1989). Yet, Emmott (1989) has predicted that Japan will not continue to be as different from other cultures as we anticipate because it is affected by human nature and market forces just like all other countries.

With all the attention focused on savings rates and Japanese foreign investments, U.S. investments overseas are going almost unnoticed. Direct foreign investment by the United States rose by $25 billion in 1988 to $351 billion. Foreign investors in the same year increased their holdings in the United States $22 billion to $350 billion. These changes can be attributed to the globalization of markets as a consequence of new information technology. The lower cost of labor is not as important a factor for overseas investment as it was in the past. The impetus is to secure foreign markets, which has led to 220 U.S. companies working on plans to establish projects overseas. Nevertheless, the scope for investing in Japan seems to be less than the prospect of investing in Europe. Although many U.S. companies are earning good profits from their Japanese investments (Figure 1.4), the relationship between Japan and the United States is intricate. Japan bought $13.7 billion worth of U.S. properties in 1989 and has moved to become the biggest investor in the United States in 1990 (Figure 1.5). However, the United States does well in some Japanese markets. Weyerhauser exports $1 billion of wood and paper products to Japan each year, and the largest fleet of Boeing 747s belongs to Japan Airlines. We tend to forget that when American Telephone and Telegraph (AT&T) was a monopoly (until 1984), it bought equipment only from its own subsidiary, Western Electric.

Cross-border alliances have become popular as competition in the telecommunications markets becomes more aggressive. They are a low-risk method for cracking global markets. Economic forces, regulatory changes, and foreign pressures are creating a more favorable climate for mergers and acquisitions in the United States, but hostile takeovers in Japan will not be possible. According to Nomura Research Institute there were 438 mergers in 1988, of which 270 were foreign acquisitions by Japanese firms. Current rules in Japan require mergers to go through domestic security houses, but the SII talks may induce changes in those rules. In the telecommunications sectors, Japanese firms are merging with foreign firms as part of the restructuring of corporate assets.

Ten years ago, the leading edge of the semiconductor industry was with the United States. In the 1980s that leadership moved to Japan, especially for state-of-the-art memory chips. Now U.S. firms are merging with their Japanese counterparts in order to gain market share. Texas Instruments announced a plan to merge with Kobe Steel in order to make logic semiconductors in Japan. AT&T

FIGURE 1.4
Comparison of Annual Percentage Growth in Gross Domestic Product: United States, Japan, and Germany

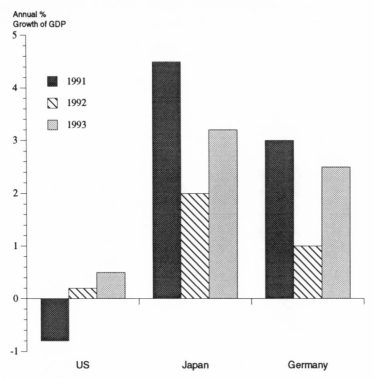

wanted to sell a broad range of chips and increase its competitiveness in the semiconductor industry, but it did not have a broad range of chips. So, in 1990 AT&T made a contract with NEC under which it will trade its computer-aided design chips for NEC's advanced logic chips. AT&T also merged with Mitsubishi for the sale of semiconductors and memory chips technology. Texas Instruments and Hitachi, Motorola, and Toshiba are other mergers within the semiconductor industry (Table 1.1). Industry observers in Japan had predicted that as the demand for chips increased in the United States, more and more U.S. manufacturers would try to strengthen their ties with their Japanese counterparts. It is a worldwide trend and appears to be pronounced in the telecommunications industry. Even Siemens, Germany's electronic giant, played student to Toshiba in order to produce the one-megabit memory chip and then produced its own next-generation semiconductor.

FIGURE 1.5
Market Share by Value of Semiconductors

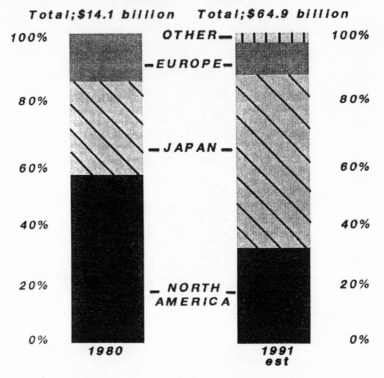

Total;$14.1 billion   Total;$64.9 billion

Source: *The Economist*, January 25, 1992, p. 66. © 1992 The Economist Newspaper Group, Inc. Reprinted with permission.

TABLE 1.1
Major Alliances in the Semiconductor Industry

U.S. Company	Japanese Company	Year
Texas Instruments	Kobe Steel	1990
AT&T	NEC	1990
Advanced Micro	Sony	1990
AT&T	Mitsubishi	1990
Intel	NMBS	1990
Texas Instruments	Hitachi	1988
Motorola	Toshiba	1986

Source: *Wall Street Journal*, March 20, 1990.

The benefits for the U.S. corporation involved differed in each alliance. They range from licenses to Japanese technology, involvement in Japanese production of memory chips, or exposure to Japanese manufacturing techniques. This proliferation of joint ventures raises questions about U.S. trade policy under which the United States is pushing for a greater share of the Japanese chip market.

Despite the use of these mergers to reduce trade tensions, Japanese corporations steadily aim to expand their share of the global market and compete as aggressively with domestic firms as with foreign rivals.

IMPLICATIONS OF TECHNOLOGICAL RIVALRY

Technorivalry is at the heart of the dispute. The United States argues that the Japanese have enjoyed the benefits of late-comer transfer of technology from the United States. But technological reciprocity is not allowed because Japanese research and development is done in corporations that are outside government control. This aspect of technonationalism surfaced when Japan's NEC was not permitted to participate in the U.S. government-supported consortium (Sematech) for manufacturing semiconductors.

Throughout the 1960s and 1970s, microelectronic technology progressed through integration and miniaturization, making the product cycle for electronic output shorter. The increase of circuit density in dynamic random access memory (DRAM) made the semiconductor industry over from small-scale integration to very large-scale integration. A decline in the cost per function of 30 percent for every doubling of chips led to tremendous gains. Prices were set below average cost. The integration between the learning curve and economies of scale encouraged U.S. companies to build their market share and increase production.

In the 1970s the Japanese were still struggling to build a competitive semiconductor industry. By the 1990s they had captured a sizable section of the U.S. and the global markets by competitive pricing, by keeping domestic prices higher than their export prices, and by exporting higher quality semiconductors with lower failure rates than their U.S. rivals. A shortfall in U.S. supplies of the 64K DRAM semiconductor, which had an inelastic demand because of its many applications, allowed the Japanese to capture as much as 70 percent of the 64K DRAM market by 1981. By the end of 1985, there was a marked over capacity in semiconductor memory chips because of large investments made by both U.S. and Japanese producers in the 256 DRAM chip, for which demand had escalated. Prices plunged worldwide. The Semiconductor Association of America appealed for protection against Japanese dumping in the U.S. market under

Section 301 of the U.S. Trade Act. The MITI responded with a rebuttal against charges of unfair trade practices.

The United States and Japan signed an agreement just before the final deadline on July 30, 1986, which meant to resolve the dispute regarding trade in semiconductors. It was agreed that Japan would stop dumping semiconductors in world markets and U.S. suppliers were promised a 12 percent share of the Japanese market.

In the United States the electronics industry has become increasingly dependent on foreign suppliers because the U.S. semiconductor industry has made insufficient investment in research, plants, and equipment. Also, few major companies who make manufacturing equipment for semiconductors remain in business in the United States, and one of these, Perkin-Elmer, is being bought by Nikon of Japan. U.S. technology is losing out in many areas of computer hardware, as can be seen in Table 1.2, which shows the decrease in the share of world markets held by the United States.

Despite the downward trend in technology development for the United States, IBM announced in February 1990 that it has built the first 16-megabit chip, and this high capacity DRAM will provide the key element in developing faster and more powerful computers. IBM was the first to manufacture the 1- and 4-megabit chips and is therefore maintaining its technological edge. It has licensed its 4-megabit technology to Micron Technology Inc. and to Sematech for the commercial market.

Fujitsu, which is now the second largest computer company in the world, has long been trying to catch up with IBM. In September 1990, Fujitsu announced a new series of mainframe computers, the largest of which can perform 600 million instructions per second. IBM announced its own new generation of mainframes one day later. This was IBM's first new mainframe generation in five years, and it was hoped that its introduction would help stem the steady erosion in IBM's worldwide market share. Hitachi bought 80 percent of National Academic Systems, which was its U.S. distributor, in April 1989. Thus, even the mainframe market is gradually being dominated by the Japanese.

TABLE 1.2
U.S. Percentage Share of World Markets

Product	1978	1988
Hard Disks	84.0	75.0
Floppy Disks	66.0	4.0
DRAMs	72.8	16.9
ASICs (customized chips)	90.0	53.0

Source: *Fortune*, January 1, 1990.

In 1988, the U.S. market for computer hardware was $50 billion, and Japan's share of this market was $2 billion. Japan's share of the personal computer market is growing, and Japanese firms have begun to assault the desktop workstations market. NEC, Fujitsu, Toshiba, Sony, and Hitachi are major suppliers in this market. Computers have become a tool for productivity — an economic lynch pin — and U.S. suppliers are relying on Japan for components in much the same manner as the U.S. electronics industry is depending on foreign suppliers of semiconductors. If there is an economic slowdown, then the Japanese computer firms may have greater resilience than the U.S. firms.

It is in the supercomputer field that this resilience is even greater. Cray Research, which is the only surviving maker of U.S. supercomputers, is running short of resources, even with an investment of $800 million. Cray's Japanese rivals are attempting to take its market.

National security concerns in the United States are colliding with national competitiveness over the definition of the term *supercomputer*. The U.S. Commerce Department defines a supercomputer as one with peak performance of 100 million floating point operations per second. The question as to whether such high-speed computers should be exported is the issue of concern. The Co-ordinating Committee on Exports to Communist Countries used to deny the export of critical technology, but national security is protected through the maintenance of technological competitiveness. It is argued that Japanese manufacturers are selling computers labeled supercomputers even though they may not be as fast or have the same peak performance.

Japan's computer industry has grown under MITI's protective barriers, which have been in place for many years. Today Japan controls the computer industry mainly because it controls the components, although it is facing competition from low-cost component suppliers in Korea, Taiwan, and Singapore. The trade imbalance is partially caused by the difficulty of maintaining a vibrant U.S. computer industry without the backing of a strong semiconductor industry.

The introduction of reduced instruction set computing (RISC) chips was regarded as the basis of a revolution in computer technology. Sun Microsystems of the United States led the way, and it is estimated that by 1993, 61 percent of all workstations around the world will be based on RISC. However, U.S. suppliers of designs for high-speed chips have licensed Japanese companies; thus, every Japanese computer supplier is adopting this technology. Sony entered the market to compete with Sun Microsystems for the lead in Unix-based workstations in Japan. The licensing of Japanese companies will also lead to U.S. designs being used for Japanese supercomputers and post–fifth generation machines.

There is a big gap in the United States-Japan trade statistics for telephone equipment and in the corresponding market share figures. The entry of Japanese switches and large business systems has been slow because there are entrenched suppliers such as AT&T and Northern Telecom Inc. (Japan Economic Institute Report #6a 1989). The Japanese are also losing ground to their Korean and Taiwanese rivals for small office systems. The deregulation of Japan's telecommunications industry and the realignment of the yen-dollar exchange rate are helping U.S. equipment makers enlarge their relatively small share of the Japanese market (Tables 1.3 and 1.4).

As computing and communications converge through digital networks and microprocessors automate everything from telephones to toasters, Japanese corporations are planning to get a better edge over their U.S. and European competitors. NEC has grown to become the world's largest seller of chips — fifth in communications and fourth in computers — although NEC's sales for 1989 of $21.3 billion were only one-third of IBM's and one-half of AT&T's sales. Koji Kobayashi, the emeritus chairman of NEC, coined the term *C & C* (computing and communications) to describe the marriage of telephones to computers in order to make instantaneous language translations. This alliance has become the new technology of integrated services digital networks, toward which telephone companies around the world are racing. Estimates show that by 1995 Japan will buy an annual supply of computers and telephones for ISDN worth $5.5 billion.

Japan's aerospace industry has lagged behind the west. When NASA put a man on the moon, the Japanese were nowhere in the picture, but now they are planning a manned presence in space early next century. An unmanned space shuttle called Hope is now under construction in order to move to manned spacecraft. Building spacecraft and its equipment is more demanding than working on the frontier of microelectronics, but it is the most value added of the high-technology systems. The estimated value of the world market for space applications by the year 2000 is $25 billion, and the Japanese want to capture 20 percent of this market by then. However, it is not a profit-making concern but rather a strategic technology that the Japanese believe should be mastered. The Japanese government has allocated $1.1 billion of its 1990 budget for space development.

In 1990 the Japanese successfully tested an advanced rocket engine, the LE-7, which is an expendable launch rocket capable of carrying a two-ton payload. In 1969 the United States and Japan signed an agreement by which the United States had a veto power over Japan's commercial launches of third country satellites. The launch of the H-2 rocket, which the National Space

TABLE 1.3
Japan's Exports of Telephone Terminal and Switching Equipment to the United States, 1983-88
(in thousands of dollars, f.o.b. value)

	1983[a]	1984	1985	1986	1987	January–October 1987	January–October 1988[b]
Key Telephone Systems	$ 30,634	$ 26,871	$28,053	$ 30,440	$ 34,054	$ 31,158	$ 16,587
Electronic Telephone Switchboards and Exchanges	36,878	37,908	18,098	23,744	21,464	16,798	
Other Telephone Switchboards and Exchanges	10,332	10,194	941	0	14	14	24,917
Desk and Wall Telephone Instruments	46,293	127,347	80,478	112,491	51,955	45,900	23,327
Other Telephone Instruments	71,121	149,248	123,452	122,021	176,342	153,378	197,708
Intercom Systems	3,724	4,389	5,129	5,147	5,869	5,303	4,064
Other Telephone Apparatus	13,691	9,833	4,639	2,206	2,395	2,261	1,458
Parts	171,358	420,953	266,346	309,348	279,809	234,287	239,544
Exports to the United States	384,030	786,743	527,137	605,397	571,902	489,099	507,604

[a]The following average annual exchange rates were used to convert the yen export figures: 1983, ¥237.52; 1984, ¥236.95; 1985, ¥240.29; 1986, ¥169.99; 1987, ¥145.90; January–October 1987, ¥148.03; and January–October 1988, ¥128.99.
[b]In 1988 Japan switched its classification system from the Customs Cooperation Council Nomenclature to the Harmonized Commodity Description and Coding System. Therefore, the product categories for 1988 do not always match exactly those for earlier years.

Source: Japan, Ministry of Finance, *Japan Exports and Imports: Commodity by Country.*

TABLE 1.4
Japan's Imports of Telephone Terminal and Switching Equipment from the United States, 1983–88
(in thousands of dollars, c.i.f. value)

	1983[a]	1984	1985	1986	1987	January–October 1987	January–October 1988[b]
Electronic Telephone Switchboards and Exchanges	$ 5,134	$ 6,927	$ 9,813	$ 14,799	$ 33,612	$ 30,136	$ 57,646
Other Telephone Switchboards and Exchanges	2	7	4	0	0	0	
Other Telephone Apparatus	1,348	4,365	6,848	3,112	5,224	4,474	4,272
Parts	30,169	43,253	59,267	78,372	87,435	68,612	88,874
Imports from the United States	36,654	54,552	75,932	96,283	126,271	103,222	150,792

[a]The following average annual exchange rates were used to convert the yen export figures: 1983, ¥237.59; 1984, ¥236.91; 1985, ¥240.17; 1986, ¥170.08; 1987, ¥146.01; January–October 1987, ¥148.09; and January–October 1988, ¥129.02.
[b]In 1988 Japan switched its classification system from the Customs Cooperation Council Nomenclature to the Harmonized Commodity Description and Coding System. Therefore, the product categories for 1988 do not always match exactly those for earlier years.

Source: Japan, Ministry of Finance, *Japan Exports and Imports: Commodity by Country.*

Development Agency of Japan (NASDA) is developing at a total cost of ¥250 billion ($1.67 billion), will free Japan from this condition. The H-2, which is a two-stage liquid fuel rocket and is comparable to the major U.S. and European rockets, is scheduled for launch in 1992.

The United States had viewed Japan's satellite development as a discriminatory trade barrier and subjected it to Super 301 procedures on June 15, 1989. Negotiations had been deadlocked for several months when the Japanese government agreed to a compromise in April 1990. They agreed to give up their former position of insisting that their commercial domestic communications satellite, the CS-4 project, be integrated into an electronic data tracking satellite project in which Japan would develop only academic research satellites with a lifespan not exceeding three years. Japan also agreed to provide free access to foreign and domestic suppliers in the procurement satellites (Table 1.5).

The telecommunications rift between Japan and the United States has been growing since the imposition of the Super 301, even though U.S. telecommunications suppliers have been able to tap certain markets in Japan. Washington's concerns about Tokyo's procurement practices reflects a broader critique of industrial targeting in Japan, under which satellites had been singled out to receive infant industry treatment.

IBM is trying to place a workstation on board Japan's module of the international space station, which is currently under development. IBM has 30 years of experience building computers for manned space flight, whereas its Japanese competitors have none. However, NASDA is allowing NEC to recommend who should build the machine; NEC is considering developing its own system. Despite its many achievements, Japan remains significantly behind the United States and Russia in space technology. U.S. technology is moving toward reusable satellites that can parachute back to earth, be refurbished, and sent aloft again. As the market for space-related equipment grows in Japan, its imports in this area are of value to U.S. corporations such as Hughes and Ford Aerospace. Hughes is already collaborating with JCSat of Japan in the construction of satellites.

As the telecommunications industry matures with new technology, price warfare will be reduced and cartelization will increase. The Federal Communications Commission will probably regulate the U.S. telecommunication industry. In Japan, a similar trend toward collusion between telecommunications firms is appearing. Japan's Fair Trade Commission is probing several Japanese firms accused of cartelized bid rigging to win a telecommunications contract from the U.S. Navy Base at Yokota, near Tokyo.

TABLE 1.5
Japanese Satellite Development

Satellite	Launch	Percent of Japan's Cost-sharing	Main Contractor
GMS	July 1977	11	NEC
CS	December 1977	23	Mitsubishi
BS	April 1978	15	Toshiba
GMS-2	August 1981	35	NEC
CS-2	February 1983	62	Mitsubishi
BS-2	January 1984	31	Toshiba
GMS-3	August 1984	32	NEC
CS-3	February 1988	80	Mitsubishi
GMS-4	November 1989	32	NEC
BS-3a*	Mid-1990	80	NEC
BS-3b*	Mid-1991	80	NEC

*Government schedule: CS — communication satellite; BS — broadcasting satellite; GMS — geostationary meteorological satellite.

ROLE OF GATT

As world services trade continues to grow from its current level of $1 trillion, the United States wants it regulated through the GATT, despite the frequent opposition from Europe and the developing countries. GATT came into the international regime for telecommunications at Punta del Este when a number of countries agreed to initiate a separate charter for trade in services. Previously, the International Telecommunication Union was the only international organization that dealt with telecommunications issues between its member countries, but technology changed its role as information exchange was replaced by information trade. Then, as trade in telematic service grew, the question arose as to whether trade rules should be imposed on international telecommunications services.

Telecommunications services, which is considered a high-priority sector by industrial and developing countries alike, will be first among six sectors to be examined by the Uruguay Round Group of Negotiations on Services (GNS). It has taken four years to establish a multilateral framework of principles and rules for different services. Priority has been given to telecommunications in the bilateral agreements that the United States had already entered into with Canada, Israel, Japan, and in the ongoing trade negotiations with Mexico. The EEC is doing the same in its green paper in preparation for a unified single market program in 1992. The GNS is giving priority consideration in the crucial final stages of the GATT talks to telecommunications in terms of cross-border services, as well as for access and use conditions for multinational companies who install their own internalized networks for communicating with their subsidiaries.

In November 1989, the U.S. Council for International Business (USCIB), composed of 300 major multinationals, proposed a new approach for a General Agreement on Trade in Services. This agreement focused on telecommunications services provided under monopoly conditions as well as those provided under competition. The USCIB further suggested that such an agreement be structurally flexible to accommodate changes in the industry occurring between this Uruguay Round and the next round of negotiations.

Telecommunications is considered a covered service, which countries subscribing to the Uruguay Round argue to be within the jurisdiction of GATT. The United States calls for an annex to the GATT charter defining public telecommunications networks and elaborating on provisions for access to the services of such networks. The annex would be a legally binding part of the agreement, applicable to data base service, electronic banking, and transborder data flows. The major elements in the annex are transparency of internal regulations, progressive liberalization of competition, market access, national treatment, and access to public networks.

However, the U.S. telecommunications giants (AT&T, MCI, etc.) have indicated that they want basic telecommunications services excluded from the current Uruguay Round talks. Basic services, which include traditional phone communication, account for the greatest share of telecommunications. The concern is that the talks could lead to a one-sided commitment by the United States to keep its basic service market open without any additional access to foreign markets for U.S. firms.

The principle of non-discrimination emphasized in the U.S. stand at the GNS talks is important for reducing trade friction between the United States and Japan. There would be ground rules for the participation of foreign suppliers in relatively closed markets, like those of Japan. Carla Hills, the USTR, says that the current talks are aimed at creating a framework for future reforms, effectively making "a table at which to negotiate."

CONCLUSION

United States-Japan trade relationships since the SII talks have had a new look and a new tone. The agreements made in April 1990 attempted to create a "level playing field in trade," and while there were proposals and counterproposals on both sides, agreement to promote structural reforms in Japan was a welcome stepping stone to improved trade relations. The SII talks, the GATT Round, mergers, and joint ventures all promise to reduce trade friction, but the question remains as to whether the $50 billion a year trade imbalance between the two countries will be reduced.

Case by case, trade reciprocity is being established in the industries named under the Super 301 clause. In most cases, Japan made concessions, and consequently the U.S. administration did not formally designate Japan for unfair trade practices under Super 301 at the end of April 1990.

The concern over the United States falling behind Japan is unfounded. The United States has not lost its global reach. Although its dominance may be declining, it is the growth and stability of productivity in the United States that will make a difference to its economic strength. Free trade is still important for productivity, and employment in trading countries and Japan, with scant natural resources, is entirely dependent on trade for maintaining its standard of living. Thus, Japan needs free trade as much as, if not more than, the United States does. The economies of Japan and the United States are interlinked, and in an age of technological dynamism in telecommunications, interdependence between the two countries grows.

Japan is a powerful model of democratic development in Asia. Its image has been altered from technobandit to miracle market. Japanese society is becoming more cosmopolitan. Television programs and the lifestyle of its younger generation follow U.S. trends. The influence of these trends will be reinforced by the acquisition of Columbia Pictures and CBS records by Sony and the more recent sale of MCA to Matsushita. Japan is committed to U.S. strategic objectives and has a western economic system, but much depends on how Japan develops a world perspective to complement its new position in the global, economic hierarchy. The reduction of trade friction should allow the United States and Japan to jointly deal with global concerns.

In the telecommunications sector, sophisticated consumer demand is a significant determinant for international trade. Demand encourages entry by many firms as we have observed in this chapter. Yet much of the success in telecommunications trade for Japan can be attributed to its economic disadvantages. The major value added to exports came from human skills and low-priced capital. Japan made its industrial structure large and homogeneous to reap economies of scale and scope, while two oil shocks only served to increase production efficiency. Innovation became the key export success, so large investments were made in research and development projects. Their competitive advantage was thus established and then maintained by building new models of electronic appliances.

Prosperity for the United States and Japan will be built on the stability of investment and trade. Both countries need to encourage alliances and free market measures to bring the developing countries within the bounds of the electronic revolution and its benefits. A direct spinoff from faster communication links is the creation of new and diverse forms of wealth. The ideals of democracy and modern capitalism have spread throughout Eastern Europe, which is a triumph for the dynamism of communication technology. The general perception of unfairness prevalent both in the United States and Japan needs to be dispelled. Care must be taken to prevent trade reciprocity, which would threaten the balance of global capital flows. Much of the tension in the United States-Japan relationship has dissipated recently, but care must be taken not to let it resurface. A world of increasingly shared power needs leadership from both the United States and Japan in this information age of spreading, pluralistic capitalism.

REFERENCES

Emmott, Bill. 1989. *The Sun Also Sets: The Limits to Japan's Economic Power.* London: Times Books.

Feldstein, Martin. 1990. "Japan's Latest Export Promotion Plan." *Wall Street Journal*, January 27.

Jussawalla, Meheroo. 1987. "The Race for Telecommunications Technology: United States versus Japan." *Telecommunications Policy*, September.

Jussawalla, Meheroo, M. Snow, and Y. Braunstein. 1988. "New Major Issues in Information Services Trade." In *Trade in Investment and Services*, edited by C. Lee and S. Naya. Boulder, CO: Westview Press.

Kreinin, Mordechai. 1988. "How Closed is Japan's Market? Additional Evidence." *World Economy*, pp. 529–42.

Stein, Herbert. 1990. "Who's Number One? Who Cares?" *Wall Street Journal*, March 1.

Wilson, Dick. 1989. "Where Trade Meets Culture: The United States, Europe, and Japan." *The Pacific Review*, vol. 2, p. 4.

2

Domestic Telecommunications Policies in the United States and Japan and Their Impact on Trade Relations

Douglas A. Conn

Linking telecommunications trade issues to changes in domestic policies is tricky. Asymmetric regulation is often the central problem of many trade negotiations between the United States and Japan. Yet while domestic policies in Japan and the United States are dynamic and progress at vastly different paces, trade talks tend to proceed in a strategic, determined fashion.

The past decade has shown the problems of high-level negotiations between two nations with different domestic regulatory and industrial approaches. A greater balance between the dynamic changes in domestic policies and the goals of international bilateral negotiations must be reached. In this chapter I argue that a balancing of domestic policy and the policymaking process in both countries must occur concomitantly with matters of trade. Many of the asymmetries that continue to exacerbate the trade imbalance have to do with the different notion of competition in the two countries. Understanding this difference can help to bring the disparate domestic policies closer to each other and ultimately can have a positive impact on trade negotiations.

This chapter will examine U.S. and Japanese domestic telecommunications policies and their importance to trade relations between the two countries. We will not try to uncover direct causal relations between domestic policies and success or failure in trade. Rather, we will analyze the structural and behavioral differences of domestic policies and discuss how their asymmetries hamper trade negotiations.

Because a major portion of this chapter deals with trade, the approach taken is more micro than macro in its outlook. It examines the trade issue from a bilateral perspective, rather than a multi-lateral perspective. As such, it does not accept managed trade as a final solution but as a component of bilateral trade negotiations between the United States and Japan.

The first section discusses the regulatory systems in the two countries, contrasting the different government bodies and the regulatory process. I assume that the reader has an understanding of the telecommunications industry in the two countries. The next section contrasts the American Telephone and Telegraph (AT&T) divestiture and Japan's consideration of a Nippon Telephone and Telegraph (NTT) divestiture, highlighting the different forces of change in their respective telecommunications sectors. Next, the results of the recent regulatory changes in the two countries and the prevailing attitudes toward competition are examined. Finally, the present trade imbalance is discussed, and some statistical evidence at the center of the trade discord, incorporating trade data from 1980–90, is presented.

U.S. AND JAPANESE REGULATORY SYSTEMS AND PROCESSES

The telecommunications regulatory environments in the United States and Japan must be compared and contrasted on two levels. The first level is the official regulatory and institutional structure, that which is perceived publicly. On this level, the two countries have a somewhat similar paternalistic structure. Regulation tends to be directed by federal agencies/ministries, although in the United States state regulatory bodies are important in the overall process. Policies encouraging competition have been introduced in both countries, and the entrance of new operators is commonplace.

The second level of comparison is the more political, or less official, approaches of policy creation and implementation. This level of analysis is more substantive in Japan. The U.S. system is one of checks and balances, lengthy public hearings and procedures, and formalized enforcement. In fact, some have argued that the U.S. process is too cumbersome (Cole and Oettinger 1978). But this is not to say that public policy is decided entirely in public fora; policy is often set between interested parties and then presented to policymakers for confirmation. The Japanese process is more hierarchical, private, and spontaneous. Enforcement of new policies can be slow. Published information on how policy is set and important statistical information are often scarce (Conn 1990).

The United States

U.S. telecommunications regulation has two dimensions: federal and state. On the federal level the primary body is the Federal

Communications Commission (FCC). It establishes rules, enforces congressional legislation, and polices the communications industry. The Communications Act of 1934 is the primary piece of legislation that established the FCC and regulates telephone companies as common carriers. This act empowers the FCC to regulate most aspects of federal telecommunications.

Congress controls the budget of the FCC and confirms its commissioners, who are nominated by the president. The president and cabinet members in the Executive Branch also appoint the head of the National Telecommunications and Information Administration (NTIA). Although it has no regulatory authority, NTIA is the conduit through which the president's positions on federal telecommunications policy are often channeled. Recently, NTIA has maintained a high profile in policymaking circles.

The U.S. Congress sets federal laws. Both the Senate and the House of Representatives have subcommittees on telecommunications that propose laws to the full Congress for consideration.

Over the past two decades, the U.S. judicial branch has effectively balanced the other two branches, verifying or overturning legislation, as well as initiating its own directives. The most important action taken by the U.S. Department of Justice — second only in its importance to the 1934 Communications Act — was the Modified Final Judgement handed down in 1982 by Judge Harold Greene of the 9th District Court in Washington, D.C. This judgment, which ended a long and protracted antitrust suit against AT&T, separated the long-distance and local telecommunications markets and effectively opened the telecommunications industry to greater competition.

State and federal regulation operate side by side and occasionally in spite of each other. This relationship is somewhat unique to the United States. Of the industrialized nations, no other nation, except possibly Canada, has placed so much authority over telecommunications regulation outside a federal or centralized body. Each of the 50 states and Washington, D.C. have their own public service commissions, which set local rates and create laws governing local operations of telecommunications companies.

In summary, the major foundations of the U.S. regulatory system are the agencies, committees, and individuals of the three branches of the federal government as well as the regulatory authorities of the 50 states. It is by many counts large and intricate, but it is open and follows established legal guidelines.

Japan

The Nihon Denshin Danwa Kohsha Hou, or NTT Law, and the Kokusai Denshin Denwa Kabushikigaisha Hou, or KDD Law, were both passed by the Japanese Diet in 1952, each creating their respective corporations. Until 1985, the laws assured the two companies a monopoly in their respective areas: NTT in the domestic market, and KDD in all international long distance. At the same time, the Ministry of Posts and Telecommunications (MPT) was formed, incorporating many of the functions of its predecessor, the Ministry of Communications (Ito and Iwata forthcoming).

MPT is the primary regulatory body in the Japanese telecommunications industry, and it maintains regulatory authority over the activities of NTT and KDD as well as over the rest of the telecommunications sector. As in other countries, NTT and KDD are regulated under common carriage principles.

The Japanese Diet and Minister's cabinet play a central role in the policymaking process. While the relationships between the Diet, cabinet, and MPT can be obfuscated by political relationships within the Japanese government, the lawmaking process is rather straightforward and structured. Generally, MPT, after discussions with industry (NTT) and union representatives, will bring a proposal to the ruling party that, when satisfied, conveys it to the full cabinet. From there, the cabinet presents it to the two houses of the Diet, which vote either for or against the new law (Sato 1990).

Along with the Ministry of Finance, which controls the government shares in NTT, the other major player in the Japanese environment has been the Ministry of International Trade and Industry (MITI). MITI is perhaps the most prestigious of Japan's ministries and was largely credited with orchestrating Japan's "economic miracle." However, its purview often conflicts with MPT's purview, especially over telecommunications equipment and computers. The infamous Telecom Wars resulted in a 1984 full-scale reorganization and reassertion of MPT's authority over telecommunications (Johnson 1986).

Another powerful constituent in the Japanese telecommunications sector is organized labor. To a much greater extent than the Communications Workers of America in the United States, NTT's union (especially after privatization) and the newly formed Rengo union (whose leader had been head of NTT's union) have important roles in the Japanese regulatory process. NTT's union is the largest in Japan's private sector and, recently, along with Rengo, has had a noticeable impact in national elections and the policy process (Sato 1990).

The Japanese Diet has sole authority to create laws that govern the telecommunications sector. Between 1952 and 1984 no new major legislative acts were passed. In 1984, two laws — the NTT Private Corporation Law and the Telecommunications Business Law — were passed. The NTT Law made NTT a privately owned company, no longer guaranteeing it a monopoly in domestic telecommunications. Unlike its regulated counterpart in the United States, NTT was permitted to offer data-processing and enhanced information services (Harris 1989). Interestingly, privatization in the telecommunications sector had been preceded by the privatization of Japan Railways, which in many ways served as a precursor for NTT.

The Ministry of Finance's role in telecommunications policy was heightened by this law. Having control over the issuance of NTT shares, the Ministry of Finance openly voiced its concern whenever new regulatory proposals or nationwide events during the 1980s were to affect the new issues.

The Telecom Business Law opened the entire Japanese telecommunications sector — local, long distance, and international — to competition. The law also created the two distinct categories of carriers: Type I, or facilities-based carriers, and Type II, or services-based carriers. Type I carriers require explicit permission from MPT. Type II carriers need only register or, in some cases, notify MPT of their intent to offer services.

The formal process of telecommunications policy setting in Japan, as in the United States, is well defined and known to interested parties. The policymaking process is, for the most part, national in scope. However, the actual influence of some of the players and relations between industry and parts of government, which go on behind the scenes, are less well-known. Also, as with many other industries in Japan, the telecommunications policymaking process is susceptible to foreign pressures. Therefore, although movement toward competition in the sector has occurred in both countries, the means of achieving it are quite different, as have been the expected outcomes. The process of divesting certain portions of each country's monopoly carrier exemplifies the different approaches toward policymaking, as discussed in the next section.

CASE FOR DIVESTITURE IN BOTH COUNTRIES

Around the world, telecommunication systems are in a state of flux. In addition to changes in consumer demand and rapidly evolving technologies, governments are relaxing regulations and allowing the telecommunications sector to resemble other sectors of their economies. This process has been referred to as normalization. Normalization has also found limited acceptance at the international level. The Uruguay Round of the General Agreement on Tariffs and Trade (GATT), when realized, will probably develop rules and procedures that take the less-progressive reforms already underway in most industrial countries, such as in the United States, the United Kingdom, and Japan, and apply them internationally.

A major component of the movement toward normalization has been the break up or privatization of government-controlled monopolies, especially telephone monopolies. Under some circumstances, this movement has taken the form of a corporate or government divestiture of the telephone monopoly carrier into separate private firms. The United States is the best example of this process. In 1984, AT&T, the sole national telephone company, divested itself of its local service carriers and kept its long-distance and international operations. Today the U.S. telecommunications sector comprises numerous companies, some large and some newer and smaller. Entrance is quite open and liberal in all but basic local service

Interestingly, Japan has seriously considered a divestiture by its monopoly carrier, NTT. The first rumblings of a divestiture were sent by the Second Provisional Commission for Administrative Reform before the enactment of the 1984 NTT Law; however, they were never considered seriously (Janisch 1988). In 1987, Japanese policymakers again considered a divestiture by NTT. However, in 1990 the Japanese government decided to postpone any final decision. Even under direct international pressure to permit greater access to its domestic markets, Japan chose to move at a more cautious pace. Japan will continue to permit, and even to encourage, competition with NTT but will not break up the monopoly carrier. The reasons behind these two divergent paths provide an interesting case study.

The United States

In the United States — the first nation to force its monopoly carrier to divest some of its operations — divestiture came about for specific economic and legal reasons. Economically, competition had already proved itself, especially in the provision of long-distance service. Confidence was also growing that the marketplace could set prices and standards and determine its output levels. Signs of discontent were sent from users and equipment providers who wished to remove government restrictions across the entire sector (Bar & Zysman 1990). On the legal side, numerous court cases had begun to challenge AT&T's monopoly status during the 1960s and 1970s. In addition, U.S. antitrust laws and a determined Department of Justice made it inevitable that the monopoly carrier, in the face of mounting competition, would be disassembled (Cole 1991).

Under the final divestiture plan, or Modified Final Judgement (MFJ), AT&T divested its 22 Bell Operating companies, which were regrouped into 7 regional holding companies (RHCs). The RHCs were assured a virtual monopoly in local service and were prohibited from offering long-distance service. Conversely, AT&T was prohibited from offering local exchange service. All cross-subsidization between long-distance carriers and local exchange carriers was effectively eliminated. The MFJ also mandated that AT&T could not inhibit local access by its competitors.

Although AT&T kept control of its equipment manufacturing arm, the newly created RHCs were prohibited from manufacturing equipment; however, they could market it. Finally, the RHCs were also prevented from offering so-called information services.

The MFJ's enforcement was left to the original judge on the case, Judge Harold Greene. To this day, he alone enforces the MFJ and hears petitions for waivers from interested parties. He has also mandated triennial reviews of the MFJ, the first of which resulted in some slight changes in information service provision by the RHCs (Cole 1991). One judge and his small staff oversee and enforce crucial regulation of an industry with total annual revenues well in excess of $150 billion.

Japan

By 1987, when Japan considered a divestiture, the conditions were different than those in the late 1970s and early 1980s in the United States. It has been said that the Japanese telecommunications sector is a decade behind that of the United States. Although this may have been true in terms of network technology or user expectations in the early 1980s, this was less the case nearly a decade later. But because Japan did not adopt divestiture as policy in 1990 speaks directly to the differences between the Japanese and U.S. regulatory systems.

Many reasons exist as to why Japan contemplated a divestiture of NTT. One reason was that NTT's initial introduction of competition had not gone far enough. Large customers were still complaining about high rates, poor service quality, and other negative effects of a concentrated industry. Pressure had been increasing for some time on MPT to remove NTT's advantage as the sole provider of national toll *and* local service. MPT and the ruling Liberal Democratic Party (LDP) also were growing increasingly concerned by the size of NTT's union and its association with Rengo. These unions were developing an inordinate amount of voting power and political clout.

A second reason for a divestiture of NTT may have been MPT's desire to consolidate its power. By reducing the size of the largest company in the industry, MPT felt that it would gain greater strength and authority over the smaller entities (Sato 1990).

Yet another reason for interest in a divestiture was the trade friction that had arisen with the United States. Foreign pressure on Japan to open its markets was mounting, and a divestiture was considered as a necessary concession if foreign entrants were to compete effectively. The U.S. influence was especially keen because of its own initial experience with deregulation and divestiture, because it had already opened its markets to foreign entrants, and the symbolic quality that telecommunications had acquired in the trade negotiations (Bar & Zysman 1990).

During the mid-1980s, MITI supported the divestiture but for entirely different reasons. MITI's efforts to assert its control of computer-based technologies and industries had suffered after the early 1980s. Deregulation, and eventually an NTT divestiture, would promote the interests of MITI's client industries (especially those not in the NTT family), while at the same time opening telecommunications to foreign competitors in order to ease trade pressures. This action would also, in the eyes of MITI, have the net effect of weakening MPT's authority (Sethia 1986).

Interestingly, the effects of three proposals considered by MPT would have varied: the first would have broken NTT into one long-distance and one local company; the second would have resulted in one long-distance carrier and several regional local operators; and the third would have broken NTT into several regional companies. The major emphasis of the first two proposals was to divide NTT along its long-distance and local operations. The third proposal, unlike that in the United States, would have divided NTT along regional lines with interconnection between the new entities.

In the end, the discussion of divestiture in Japan was quietly postponed. The Japanese government did not entirely abandon the idea, but it will not officially revisit it until 1995. Until 1995, MPT will continue to introduce controlled competition in the telecommunications sector. It has also placed a renewed emphasis on opening the Japanese long-distance, local, and international services markets to greater competition.

At the time of its decision, the government also introduced new measures to advance existing competition. It has proposed to divide NTT along its long-distance and local companies to prevent, among other things, the possibility of one side of the business subsidizing the revenues of the other. It is also pushing a more equitable interconnection policy between NTT and the new carriers, seeking open access to the national network for all carriers. NTT has also had to divest itself of its cellular subsidiary, which will, as a private company, compete in a more open market (KDD 1991).

There were a number of clear reasons for the government's decision to postpone a divestiture — some were sectoral but many were nonsectoral. First, the Japanese stock market had been weakened like most others in the world. In light of this, the Ministry of Finance effectively blocked an NTT divestiture for fear that it would further lower NTT's stock price and destabilize the domestic financial markets. As a 67 percent owner of NTT's stock, the Ministry of Finance's opinion carried tremendous weight (Sato 1990).

Since the early 1980s, Japanese politics have also played an important role in preventing the breakup of NTT. Through time, only the MPT supported the divestiture. MITI became especially worried about the reduced research and development power of a divested

NTT, which would weaken the nation's international competitiveness. Consequently, the role of telecommunications in the government's industrial policy was considered too important to dismiss.

The ruling LDP also eventually withdrew its support. The LDP contained different factions, some of which supported a breakup and others that were against it. As a result, those against the breakup became the majority. The celebrated Recruit scandal and resignation of former NTT Chair Shinto was a major reason for the change of support. MPT saw NTT's involvement in the scandal as another example of a dominant firm operating inefficiently and continued to press for a divestiture. However, the scandal helped to shift attention away from a divestiture ruling, especially as the prolabor Socialist Party gained in popularity and NTT's stock embarked on a precipitous decline.

Of course, NTT itself had officially been opposed to any form of a divestiture. As of March 1990, Haruo Yamaguchi, president and chief executive officer of NTT, publicly stated that an NTT breakup would raise local rates and the network "would suffer, much like in the United States" (Sanger 1990).

The decision to delay a divestiture was for many reasons, some of which were within the Japanese government's control. However, the mood in Japan appears to be that the issue of divestiture, or other type of NTT reorganization, cannot be swept under the rug. It will resurface in time for a 1995 decision. The question that remains is who will be its most ardent supporter and will they succeed? The strong possibility exists that MPT will continue to make evolutionary steps, much like the 1991 structural separation of NTT's mobile communications business. The end result may be a less-centralized but still consolidated holding company.

Unlike in the United States, Japan does not have a strong legal system or a fragmented political constituency (unions, users, equipment manufacturers, etc.). Because of these differences, the timing of policy changes will remain, perhaps, the most important factor in the Japanese telecommunications sector.

IMPACT OF REGULATORY CHANGE IN THE UNITED STATES AND JAPAN

Regulatory change occurred in Japan and the United States during the 1980s but in different forms. One form was the more drastic approach of the United States, and the other form was the more measured evolution of Japan. Competition is being introduced into telecommunications, both domestically and internationally, in nations from Australia to Hong Kong, from Canada to Germany. Pressure will continue to build from neighboring and distant nations to open markets — a type of exportation of competition.

In the United States and Japan the national competition policies did not include competition in local service areas; these remain monopolies. Economists point to the theory of natural monopoly, while policymakers point to the notion of universal service to support this exception. Both nations have concentrated instead on opening all other parts of the sector with different results.

Japan and other nations fear the decline of their telecommunications systems as a result of a divestiture. Given the experiences of the United States, these fears are unwarranted. In fact, many problems predicted for the AT&T divestiture, such as soaring prices and users dropping off the network, did not materialize.

By most measures Japanese competition policy has also been a success. Many in Japan believe that their approach will achieve the same results as those in the United States, but without a single tumultuous breakup.

The United States

The U.S. divestiture has been successful by most measurements. The telecommunications industry has become one of the fastest growing sectors of the U.S. economy as a result of divestiture. Long-distance rates have decreased, local phone rates have risen in step with inflation (see Table 2.1), and prices for network and customer equipment have steadily declined. Total expenditures on research and development have increased since divestiture, and the number of long-distance and private line carriers has risen. The privatization of networks has resulted in more rapid deployment of telecommunications technology and greater diversity of service offerings. Competition has substantially increased, due in part to the divestiture and

TABLE 2.1
Telephone Prices
(Annual Rate of Change in Percent)

	Local	Intrastate Toll	Interstate Toll	Access
1984	17.2	3.6	−4.3	—
1985	8.9	0.6	−3.7	−8.1
1986	7.1	0.3	−9.5	−14.3
1987	3.3	−3.0	−12.4	−21.7
1988	4.5	−4.2	−4.2	−8.5
Total	41.0	−2.7	−34.1	−52.6

Source: FCC Price Index Study, 1989. From Bruce Egan and Leonard Waverman. 1991. "The State of Competition in Telecommunications." In *After the Breakup: Assessing the New Post AT&T Divestiture Era*, Barry Cole, ed. New York: Columbia University Press.

in part to the removal by the government of entry barriers and cross-subsidization (see Tables 2.2 and 2.3). Although it is difficult to ascertain if service quality improved, we know that it has not suffered. Penetration has stayed at its consistently high levels (Cole 1991).

Some negative effects do exist. Many argue that the divestiture compounded the already growing trade deficit, especially in high-technology industries. By opening U.S. markets before its major trading partners had even contemplated doing the same, the United States started a dangerous trend. According to the American Electronics Association a $1 billion telecommunications trade surplus existed in 1980. By 1984, the first year after divestiture, this surplus had plummeted to a $700 million trade deficit and has continued to drop ever since (Bar & Zysman 1990). Many other factors also account for this drop, but free entry to domestic markets without reciprocation exacerbated the problem.

TABLE 2.2
Interexchange Carriers Market Shares
(Percent Revenue)

	1984	1985	1986	1987	1988
AT&T	90.96	89.35	84.42	82.28	78.09
MCI	5.10	6.18	8.31	9.20	11.33
US Sprint	3.24	3.27	5.42	6.24	7.51
NTN	—	0.36	0.81	1.35	2.21
Allnet	0.70	0.84	1.04	0.92	0.87

Source: Annual reports, company data. From Bruce Egan and Leonard Waverman. 1991. "The State of Competition in Telecommunications." In *After the Breakup: Assessing the New Post AT&T Divestiture Era*, Barry Cole, ed. New York: Columbia University Press.

TABLE 2.3
AT&T Share of the Interstate Market
(Percent, End of Year)

	Premium Minutes	All Minutes
1984	94	80
1985	88	77
1986	79	73
1987	74	70
1988	69	67

Source: *FCC Report on Interstate Switched Access*, March 1989. From Bruce Egan and Leonard Waverman. 1991. "The State of Competition in Telecommunications." In *After the Breakup: Assessing the New Post AT&T Divestiture Era*, Barry Cole, ed. New York: Columbia University Press.

Japan

Japanese deregulation and competition policies have had remarkable and immediate success. Japan has encouraged the proliferation of value-added network providers. By July 1990, 64 facilities-based competitors were operating alongside NTT, and there were 872 Type II carriers (Sato 1990).

Generally, in the late 1980s, local rates did not rise, even as long-distance and international rates fell rapidly. New services were introduced by both NTT and its competitors (Janisch 1990). Competition has spurred NTT to innovate and cut costs more rapidly. In addition, NTT has recently agreed to certain concessions in light of the postponed discussions of divestiture. These concessions should increase competition in additional segments of the market.

International services in Japan also represent an area where competition policies have made significant positive impact. Two new carriers, International Telecom Japan (ITJ) and International Digital Communications (IDC) are now competing with KDD. The most effective weapon of the new carriers is their lower price. Since 1985, price competition in the international long-distance market has caused KDD to lower its rates by some 50 percent, even with the controlled competition established by MPT (KDD 1990) (see Tables 2.4 and 2.5). Among countries where competition in international long-distance exists, Japan can be considered the most competitive in the world. In fact, KDD's competitors had captured 15 percent of all outgoing traffic just six months after their start-up. Interestingly, the two major competitors to KDD are owned by many of the largest users in Japan. Also, presubscription is not necessary for service (Staple 1990; KDD Annual Report 1990).

Given the continued close regulation of NTT and tightly managed entry conditions by MPT, the new common carriers (NCCs) competing with NTT were expected to have realized greater than 20 percent of Japan's domestic traffic by late 1990. This figure represents only

TABLE 2.4
Comparison of International Telephone Rates in Japan
(in Yen)

	KDD	ITJ, IDC
Prior to Competition	890	—
November 1989 (KDD Rate Reduction)	730	680
April 1990 (KDD Rate Reduction)	680	680
September 1990 (ITJ, IDC Rate Reduction)	680	670

Note: Rates based on three-minute call, standard time, between Japan and the United States.

Source: KDD America

TABLE 2.5
Comparison of International Leased Circuit Rates in Japan
(in Yen)

	KDD	ITJ, IDC
Voice Grade	590,000	550,000
64 Kbits	890,000	830,000
256 Kbits	2,190,000	2,040,000
1.5 Mbits	7,020,000	6,553,000

Note: Rates based on standard circuit between the United States and Japan. ITJ and IDC rates are generally 7 percent less than KDD rates.

Source: KDD America.

local competitors in major Japanese cities and in the Tokyo-Osaka long-distance corridor. (The Tokyo-Osaka corridor represents nearly 80 percent of all traffic in Japan [Janisch 1990].) But competition in Japan came quickly because of the concentration of users within the country and the latent demand, not solely because of MPT control over the sector.

Japan's competition policy has its drawbacks though. The primary drawback, which was not fully addressed because of the postponement of divestiture, was how to handle NTT's ability to compete. The NCCs will continue to gain market share under the current regulatory conditions, and NTT will continue to watch its position decline. In 1989 alone, NTT's operating income was down by 11 percent, and its net income per share was down 1.3 percent. At the same time though, NTT continued to subsidize local rates with long distance. It enjoyed regulatory protection through favorable interconnection terms and access charges as determined by MPT. Given this imbalance, we must wonder when and how MPT will deal with the inconsistency of its approach with NTT. Perhaps, as with AT&T in the United States, NTT will initially remain regulated and will eventually have more and more regulations lifted.

Japanese and U.S. goals of an effective competition policy appear to be similar. Japan has learned from U.S. mistakes in some areas, such as the opening of its markets to foreign competitors without reciprocity. However, Japan's half-regulatory, half-competitive control over NTT and its behind-the-scenes approach toward policy creation are quite different from those in the United States. Also important is the role of the keiretsu, or closely tied supplier networks, which encourage stability and longer-term relations in the domestic market. These factors have slowed the development of competitive services provisions and competitive sourcing for network equipment. It is currently in the Japanese government's best interest to retain oversight of NTT; it is an effective tool in fiscal, industrial, labor, and, of course, telecommunications policy. The battle over NTT's status will most likely last for some time, especially since NTT has itself now taken on a symbolic quality in domestic government policy and in international trade negotiations.

UNITED STATES-JAPAN TRADE IN TELECOMMUNICATIONS

In what have the different approaches toward competition policy resulted? Both countries have more competitors, lower prices, renewed growth, and more rapid deployment of new technology. However, the U.S. trade deficit has continued to grow rapidly because of strong imports and the lack of entry to Japanese and other markets. In Japan, each strategic sector of the telecommunications market has seen only one foreign supplier (Vietor & Yoffie 1990). In contrast, the U.S. market is open to foreign suppliers of equipment.

The highly political nature of telecommunications, combined with the disparate regulatory regimes of the United States and Japan, can produce unusual patterns of trade. Comparative advantage does not take hold in telecommunications trade because of regulatory and political barriers. Japanese policies that seek to protect the domestic market have resulted in virtual vertical integration, effectively excluding competitors from entering the domestic market (Vietor & Yoffie 1990). MPTs stronghold of NTT and the rest of the telecommunications sector is the linchpin of this strategy.

In the past, national telecommunications policy had been the affairs of technocrats at the post, telephone, and telegraph (PTT). Given their position, they could afford to pay little attention to the international consequences of their decisions. But this dynamic has changed dramatically, not only because of foreign pressure but because of rapid changes to the evolution of telecommunications networks caused by shifts in consumer demand (Noam forthcoming).

Trade talks during the 1980s have all to often failed for many of these reasons. The 1981 United States-Japan Agreement on NTT Procurement and the Understanding of Japan's Interconnect Market initially had little impact on trade in equipment between the United States and NTT. The procurement practices of NTT remained slow and cumbersome. To complicate matters, only the largest U.S. firms attempted sales to Japan, and many of these firms offered less than state-of-the-art equipment with the expectation that the agreement would pressure the Japanese to accept all product offered (U.S. General Accounting Office 1983). These trade agreements were failures in both directions.

Not all negotiated agreements have failed. Japan's consideration and implementation of deregulation was the subject of intense negotiations with the United States in 1984–85. One result was an increased attention to competition policy, which some believe directly benefited U.S. firms. On the services side, both countries have permitted foreign participation and ownership. Still, as of 1989, Japan had total worldwide exports in telecommunications equipment of $18.4 billion and imports of $1.3 billion (Sato 1990).

The 1988 U.S. Trade Act, which included a special provision on telecommunications trade, was the U.S. government's response to the continued trade imbalance. The market oriented sector specific negotiations of the mid- to late-1980s had proven slow, producing few immediate results. The act's special trade representative identified Japan as a priority country in 1989, and subsequently some breakthroughs were reached in the cellular market. However, the overall imbalance continues to remain high (Vietor and Yoffie 1990).

Here, briefly, are some of the more pertinent statistics on equipment and services trade. The total U.S. deficit for all electronics-based products was at $25 billion in 1988, having dropped from a surplus of approximately $5 billion in 1983 (Cole 1991). The trade deficit from 1981 to 1988 for the United States in telecommunications grew, on average, by approximately $430 million per year (see Table 2.6).

TABLE 2.6
U.S. Telecommunications Equipment Trade
($ million)

	Trade Balance	Year-to-Year Change
1981	817	
		-542
1982	275	
		-793
1983	-518	
		-633
1984	-1,151	
		-715
1985	-1,866	
		-164
1986	-2,030	
		-520
1987	-2,550	
		-58
1988	-2,608	
		623
1989	-1,935	

Note: 1989 figure would have been approximately -2,300 had accounting methods used in previous years not been revised.

Source: Office of Telecommunications, International Trade Administration, U.S. Commerce Department. From Michael Baudhuin. 1991. "Issues of International Trade." In *After the Breakup: Assessing the New Post AT&T Divestiture Era*, Barry Cole, ed. New York: Columbia University Press.

In 1982, the United States was exporting approximately $2.1 billion in telecommunications equipment and importing nearly $3 billion. In 1987, the United States was exporting nearly $4 billion and importing more than $6 billion. In 1982, Japan was exporting more than $1 billion in telecommunications and importing less than $100 million. In 1987, Japan was exporting more than $3 billion in telecommunications and importing less than $500 million (Vietor & Yoffie 1990). These data should be contrasted with foreign procurement by NTT, which, when taken alone, has shown a marked increase in the 1980s (see Table 2.7). Approximately half of all Japan's imports in telecommunications were through NTT procurements.

Trade in public telecommunications services presents a somewhat different picture. Since 1987, well before the introduction of competition in international service, Japan had been experiencing a 30 percent outbound traffic growth. All indices indicate it will continue along these lines. In the United States, 1 percent of all calls placed are international. In the United Kingdom, 2 percent of all calls placed are international. But in Japan, only 0.15 percent of all calls are international, indicating the potential for growth, especially with the rise in facsimile and other data transmission. As it now stands, Japan ranks only tenth in terms of international traffic. Continued growth may cause the traffic surplus between Japan and its major trading partners to shrink, the net effect being the reduction not removal of overall service deficit figures (Staple 1990).

Table 2.4 shows the countries with deficits and surpluses in total minutes of telephone traffic in 1988. In telephone traffic, the United States and Canada are imbalanced, and Japan is almost at parity. Table 2.8 shows the potential for growth in certain countries. Given

TABLE 2.7
Foreign Procurement by NTT
($ million)

	Total Foreign	United States Only
1981	19	17
1982	44	34
1983	147	132
1984	144	130
1985	167	145
1986	232	209
1987	275	249
1988*	323	289
1989*	352	318

*Does not include NTT Data Corp.

Source: NTT America.

TABLE 2.8
1988 Trade Balance in Public Voice Minutes of
Telecommunications Traffic

	Outgoing	Incoming	Balance	Deficit/Surplus as Percent of Total Traffic
United States	5,325	3,155	(2,170)	(25.6)
West Germany	2,479	2,080	(399)	(8.8)
United Kingdom	1,729	1,814	85	2.4
France	1,570	1,690	120	3.7
Japan	529	553	24	2.2
Australia	415	331	(84)	(11.3)
Mexico	211	504	(293)	40.9
Singapore	152	126	(26)	(9.3)

Source: Gregory C. Staple. 1990. *The Global Telecommunications Traffic Boom: A Quantitative Brief on Cross-Border Markets and Regulation.* International Institute for Communications.

Japan's size and gross national product per capita, the potential for growth in outgoing traffic is enormous. This, in fact, has been proven by the tremendous growth of ITJ and IDC, the two new international carriers in Japan. Finally, in a direct comparison, as shown in Tables 2.9 and 2.10, the United States had an outflow of some 232

TABLE 2.9
Major Telecommunications Correspondents of the
United States Measured by Public Voice Minutes of
Telecommunications Traffic

	Outgoing	Market Share in Percent
Canada	1,075	20
United Kingdom	485	9
Mexico	470	9
West Germany	367	7
Japan	232	4
France	145	3
Italy	128	2
South Korea	122	2
Dominican Republic	119	2
Colombia	108	2

Note: The above top 10 correspondents represent 61 percent of total outgoing traffic from the United States.

Source: Gregory C. Staple. 1990. *The Global Telecommunications Traffic Boom: A Quantitative Brief on Cross-Border Markets and Regulation.* International Institute for Communications.

million minutes of telephone traffic to Japan in 1988, and Japan had 145 million minutes of telephone traffic to the United States (Staple 1990).

TABLE 2.10
Major Telecommunications Correspondents of Japan Measured by Public Voice Minutes of Telecommunications Traffic

	Outgoing	Market Share in Percent
United States	145	27
South Korea	72	14
Taiwan	56	11
Hong Kong	42	8
United Kingdom	33	6
West Germany	17	3
Australia	16	3
Singapore	16	3
France	10	2
Thailand	8	2

Note: The above top 10 correspondents represent 78 percent of total outgoing traffic from Japan.

Source: Gregory C. Staple. 1990. *The Global Telecommunications Traffic Boom: A Quantitative Brief on Cross-Border Markets and Regulation.* International Institute for Communications.

CONCLUSIONS

Competition policies in the United States and Japan have taken different paths. The AT&T divestiture was a relatively large-scale reorganization of the U.S. telecommunications sector. The Japanese efforts to introduce competition in the 1980s were more measured. These divergent approaches parallel the overall characteristics of the policymaking processes in the two countries. They are also an integral part of the parameters within which both sides negotiate trade issues.

Two primary problems remain as a legacy from the deregulatory policies of the 1980s: for the United States, the growing trade deficit; for the Japanese, the inequitable treatment of NTT vis-à-vis its new competitors. Overall success in U.S. competition policies is seriously impeded by trade imbalances and a growing deficit. Telecommunications is a global industry; domestic markets are directly affected by overseas developments. Whether narrowsighted or not, the AT&T divestiture warrants that the United States continue to seek more open markets with its major trading partners. The success of certain domestic policies, especially in equipment manufacturing, hinge on this.

However, many in Japan view the accelerated process of deregulation in the United States as a mistake. Some have argued that the U.S. approach was too hasty and remains fragmented; the United States should have taken more intermediate steps to implement its competition policies and made more efforts to promote a single national telecommunications policy (Harris 1989). But, in terms of its competition policy, Japan itself has yet to define its final stages of a national telecommunications policy. Japan's goal of a competitive telecommunications sector is seriously hampered by its imbalanced approach toward NTT.

Trade negotiations in telecommunications have tended to succeed as of late on a case-by-case basis (satellites, cellular telephones, etc.) rather than a sectoral or even market level. This tactic currently is enjoying widespread support in the United States, though with only near term consequences. Both governments are forced to cater to the needs of a small group or single firm, and larger issues remain unresolved.

Trade talks, or other bilateral talks on telecommunications, should concentrate equally on opening individual markets or on pursuing the interests of individual firms, as well as specific discussions of effective competition policies and their benefits to consumers and the domestic economy. Ultimately, more fruitful results may result when government and industry in both countries pay equal attention to the differences in their domestic policies.

REFERENCES

Aronson, Jonathan David and Peter F. Cowhey. 1988. *When Countries Talk: International Trade in Telecommunications Services.* Cambridge, MA: Ballinger.

Bar, Francois and John Zysman. 1990. "The Unbalanced Triad." In *Impacts, Policies and Future Perspectives: Promotion of Mutual Understanding Between Europe and Japan*, edited by F. Meyer-Krahmer, J. Mueller and B. Preissi, pp. 216–29. New York: Springer-Verlag.

Cole, Barry, ed. 1991. *After the Break-up: Assessing the New Post AT&T Divestiture Era.* New York: Columbia University Press.

Cole, Barry and Mal Oettinger. 1978. *Reluctant Regulators: The FCC and the Broadcast Audience.* Reading, MA: Addison-Wesley.

Conn, Douglas. 1990. "Divestiture in Telecommunications." *Hong Kong Economic Journal*, October 23 (in Chinese and English).

Harris, Robert. 1989. "Telecommunications Policy in Japan: Lessons for the United States." *California Management Review*, Vol. 31, No. 3, Spring, pp. 113–31.

Ito, Yoichi and Atsushi Iwata. Forthcoming. "Historical Review of Japanese Telecommunications Policies." In *Pacific Basin Telecommunications*, edited by Eli M. Noam, Seisuke Komatsuzaki, and Douglas A. Conn.

Janisch, Hudson. 1988. "Developments in Japanese Telecommunications." Working Paper 1988-44, Faculty of Law, University of Toronto, December 12.

＿＿. 1990. "Telecom Liberalization in Japan." Presented at Gartner

Group/Transition Group Second Annual Canadian Telecommunications Conference, Montreal, May.

Japan Economic Institute. 1991. *The Outlook for United States-Japan Trade Relations: An Interview with S. Linn Williams of USTR.* January 11, JEI Report No. 1A, Washington, DC: Japan Economic Institute.

Johnson, Chalmers. 1986. *MITI, MPT and the Telecom Wars: How Japan Makes Policy for High Technology.* Working Paper 21, Berkeley Roundtable on the International Economy, University of California, September.

KDD Annual Report. 1990. March 31.

KDD. 1991. "Regulatory and Industry Development in Japan." Internal document. Tokyo.

Noam, Eli. Forthcoming. "The Three Stages of Telecommunications Evolution." In *Pacific Basin Telecommunications,* edited by Eli M. Noam, Seisuke Komatsuzaki, and Douglas A. Conn.

NTT Annual Report. 1990. March 31.

Sanger, David E. 1990. "Nippon Telephone Split Delayed." *New York Times,* April 2, p. D4.

Sato, Harumasa. 1990. "Recent Developments in Japanese Telecommunications." Presented at *Dividing PTTs in Regulatory and Operating Bodies: Experiences and Problems in Telecommunications Abroad,* The Center for Telecommunications and Information Studies, Columbia University, October.

Sethia, Nirmal. 1986. *The Challenge of the Japanese Telecommunications Market.* Report No. 2, Center for Telecommunications Management, University of Southern California, January.

Staple, Gregory C. 1990. *The Global Telecommunications Traffic Boom: A Quantitative Brief on Cross-Border Markets and Regulation.* International Institute for Communications.

U.S. General Accounting Office. 1983. *Assessment of Bilateral Telecommunications Agreements with Japan.* NSIAD-84-2, October 7. Washington, D.C.: U.S. General Accounting Office.

Vietor, Richard and David Yoffie. 1990. *Global Competitiveness in Telecommunications.* Harvard Business School Working Paper, draft, March 2.

3

Political Aspects of United States-Japan Trade Conflicts

Fumiko Mori Halloran

All foreign policy issues in any country are a reflection of domestic political issues. Negotiations over semiconductors, satellites, and supercomputers between Japan and the United States reflect the interest of domestic industries, government policies, legislators' behavior, and coverage of the issues by the press. Each interest group exercises political pressures to gain its objective in its own country, which results in complex interactions both within each country and between the two countries.

Between Japan and the United States the nature of economic conflict has been changing from disputes over trade to contention over access to financial markets and the way both countries conduct business and manage their economies. The Structural Impediments Initiative (SII) negotiations demonstrated that. At the bottom of these disputes are two issues: the persistent trade surplus by Japan against the United States and the U.S. perception that Japan has been an unfair trading partner in nontariff barriers and markets closed to foreign imports.

Surface debates on both sides are about numbers, theories, and trade policies, which often signify something deeper. The United States is frustrated that Japan has been a free rider in defense and has a vague fear that Japan might one day dominate the United States by its economic power. The Japanese are often indignant that U.S. businesses push the Japanese around and that the United States singles out Japan as a scapegoat for their own problems. Both the United States and Japan are mindful that they were enemies in World War II four decades ago.

This confrontation, then, is political, and all trade issues are used as tools by both countries. Economists and trade experts may not agree, but the way in which individual trade disputes are solved indicates that political solutions are needed to solve political issues, even if they are expressed as trade issues. In other words, trade issues have escalated to political issues with alarming outcries from both countries.

In this chapter, I will first describe briefly how various political pressures about trade disputes are exerted on policymakers in both countries. Then, I will describe the different characteristics in the negotiating styles of the United States and Japan. Finally, I will conclude by suggesting what measures could be taken to lessen, if not remove, unnecessary obstacles to a constructive partnership.

POLITICAL PRESSURES ON TRADE POLICYMAKING

In the United States, trade policymakers from the White House on down are influenced by two U.S. characteristics: an instinct for checks and balances and a dynamic interaction between competing pressure groups. This influence is clear in the executive and legislative branches. The president makes the final decision, but he does not have dictatorial power. The president's cabinet may be divided among secretaries who represent departments with diverse and often conflicting interests.

In United States-Japan relations, the U.S. State Department tends to look at the relationship in overall terms, its priority being to keep the alliance in good order. The Department of Defense and the National Security Council have a similar outlook, as they have vital interests in keeping a close security alliance with Japan. However, when a trade dispute affects national security, they become tough. The U.S. Department of Commerce, however, is often aggressive in achieving specific results for a specific industry or specific companies that have complaints against Japan. While the U.S. Trade Representative (USTR) may form an alliance with the Department of Commerce on specific issues, it also has an interest in working with Japan on global and multinational negotiations.

Presently, the Department of Agriculture is attracting attention because of its criticism that U.S. farmers cannot export rice to Japan. Rice, while symbolizing unfair Japanese trade practices from the U.S. point of view, has become the symbol for protecting Japanese farmers and the Japanese way of life.

The U.S. Treasury is concerned with the yen-dollar exchange rate. Collaboration with other industrial nations, including Japan, on currency realignment has an overall effect on international trade. Although the U.S. Treasury usually does not concern itself much with specific trade disputes, it initiated the idea of SII, as its officials recognized the need to press for basic changes in Japanese industries. Their conclusion was derived from a concern that in 1985 the United States-Japan trade imbalance persisted. The State Department, the Office of Management and Budget, the Council of Economic Advisors, and the Justice Department joined the Treasury to focus on procedures that would lift barriers rather than on the specific objectives that the Commerce Department and USTR pursued.[1] The division among government agencies on trade issues reflects not only ideological differences, such as free trade versus protectionism, but also turf battles as to who takes the lead in international negotiations.

The Office of USTR, which was created by the Congress in 1962 as the Office of the Special Representative for Trade Negotiations, is designated as the lead trade negotiator for the United States. The USTR is supposed to present a united front after reviewing different views and considering all possible options from various interest groups. Yet, as its competition with the Commerce Department indicates, the USTR is under constant pressure from other agencies and Congress that are determined to influence U.S. trade policy. The clout of the USTR often depends on the political support the trade representative gets from the White House and the Congress.

The U.S. Congress exercises its influence on the administration's policy in several ways. Members call for hearings by various committees to highlight major issues, and they pass resolutions that are not binding but that indicate which way the wind is blowing and what kind of legislation may be in the making. Congressional legislation, such as the Super 301 provision of the 1988 Omnibus Trade and Competitiveness Act, often passes despite resistance from the administration. So far, the Reagan and Bush administrations have been advocating a policy of free trade that often clashes with an increasingly protectionist Congress.

In Washington, D.C. most legislative work is done by staff members who are not elected officials. They often shape their bosses' thinking with their expertise and political skills. The negotiations, bargaining, and compromises among not only legislators but their staffs are little understood outside Congress and Washington, D.C. In the process, legislation that was conceptually extreme at first is often watered down to middle road and more realistic terms as it passes through committee hearings and onto the floor of either house.

Throughout this process, congressional members and staff are approached by representatives of special interest groups: lawyers, lobbyists, foreign agencies, think-tank experts, academics, and others interested in single issues. Foreign representatives, such as ambassadors, also state their positions. In the event that trade issues are brought to court, some individuals present friend-of-the-court opinions.

Members of these groups are often seen waiting outside meeting rooms on Capitol Hill, where conferences are held to work out differences between Senate and House versions of legislation. Congressional staff members seek the help of representatives of special interests in shaping the bills because the lobbyists and specialists often know more about the details and implications than do the staff members. In this atmosphere the line between enemy and friend is unclear, and the success or failure of a piece of legislation depends on the negotiations and compromises among these groups.

Finally, press reports on trade issues have a direct and often telling effect on the perceptions on both policymakers and the public. The media can be divided into print (news agencies, newspapers, and weekly magazine) and electronic (television and radio). In their approach to reporting, the media can also be divided between straight reporting and news analysis, columns, and editorials. Journals on foreign policy, economic matters, and national security, which are read by specialists, should also be included. Generally, the influence of these journals is limited compared with that of the general press, particularly that of television. Nevertheless, articles written by specialists for other specialists often have some influence and that, in turn, may shape the thinking of policymakers for whom these specialists serve as advisers.

How information on trade issues is generated, analyzed, and distributed and how it influences journalists and policymakers is a topic for research itself. Policymakers use the press by leaking information. The press finds news that policymakers do not want known. Reading newspaper accounts and reacting to them, policymakers make statements and appear on television news talk shows, which in turn creates more news. In this high-technology electronic age, the speed with which such information is transmitted — not only within the United States but in Japan, and back and forth between them — certainly politicizes the relationship.

The president of the United States has to weigh every possible option presented by many, diverse interest groups. The prime minister of Japan also faces formidable interest groups but has far less power to deal with them. One advantage the prime minister has over the president is that the prime minister can count on his party's support to override opposition parties. He is head of the majority party in parliament. In the United States, a president is elected separately from legislators. He may be in a position, as is President Bush, to face a Congress in which the majority is held by the opposition party.

But the Japanese parliament is not based on the two-party system as is that in the United Kingdom. The ruling Liberal Democratic Party (LDP) has been in power since 1955, which makes it difficult to generate strong policy debates between the opposing parties.

The LDP is a loose coalition of factions headed by senior leaders who play tough political games, particularly on the issue of who will succeed the current prime minister. The LDP members' ideology ranges from hawkish to dovish, from protector to free trader, and from conservative to liberal. The only ideology that binds them together is that they are against communism/socialism and are for capitalism.[2]

As in the United States, the Japanese legislator's top priority is his or her constituency. If the livelihood of a district is at stake because of trade issues, a legislator will try to protect the local interest. Many legislators cannot afford to be foreign policy experts or to think of long-term national interests because of an immediate need to win the next election. Thus, trade issues may face political obstacles as they become localized and emotional.

At the national level, key members of committees in the National Diet, particularly committees in the more powerful House of Representatives, have cultivated close ties with certain industries. Protecting such industries, who may lose business as a result of trade agreements with the United States, hampers negotiations.[3]

Compared with their U.S. counterparts, Japanese legislators lack staff, which forces them to rely on the bureaucracy in the executive branch to draft legislation. In the U.S. Congress, legislators rely on large congressional staffs who are experts on specific issues. Every representative and senator, in addition to a personal staff, has access through committee assignments to the staffs of these committees and to agencies such as the Congressional Research Service and the General Accounting Office.

Japanese legislators have noting comparable, having only a small personal staff. The National Diet Library's research staff provides similar services, but they are not used as extensively as the services used by U.S. legislators. Thus, the Japanese bureaucracy fills the void, which often creates tension between legislators and bureaucrats.

The Japanese bureaucracy recruits from the best and the brightest in the nation and is protected by a civil service tradition that does not permit much manipulation on political appointments. As a result, each ministry has an institutional memory, a tight team, and a sense of mission in furthering the national interest. But tradition since the nineteenth century has also created an inflexibility that delays swift political solutions.

Competition for leadership in international trade negotiations is fierce among government agencies, as in the United States. The Ministry of Foreign Affairs, such as the U.S. Department of State, tends to see United States-Japan relations in the overall context of alliance. But, as with the State Department, the Ministry of Foreign

Affairs suffers from the lack of a domestic power base, which leads to a weaker position in political fights.

In contrast, the Ministry of International Trade and Industry (MITI) has a powerful influence on domestic industries and their trade behavior. The Finance Ministry has tight control over financial institutions. The Ministry of Agriculture, Fisheries, and Forestry is backed by farmers, who in turn support the ruling party in elections.

Private businesses, both as industries and individual companies, approach bureaucracy and legislators to make their cases in trade crises. They do so through individual contact and national and regional organizations. As Tokyo is not only the nation's political center but also its business center, where almost all corporate headquarters are situated, formal and informal contacts between government officials and business executives are many and intense. This close relationship draws both envy and criticism from U.S. policymakers as the general pattern of government-business relationships in the United States is adversarial. The relationships make it difficult for the United States to agree on a united, comprehensive trade policy when they deal with Japanese negotiators.

The Japanese government-business relationship, however, is by no means harmonious. It is true that the intent of both sides in Japan is to reach a consensus before the official delegation meets its U.S. counterpart, but the process is time-consuming, tense, and sometimes acrimonious. In 1981 when Japan issued self-imposed restraints on automobile exports to the United States, the split between MITI, which pushed for restraints, and the auto makers, who strongly opposed them, was played out in public. In the end, the government prevailed, and the self-restraint policy is still exercised by Japan, largely for political reasons.

Japan does not have a law that requires persons of influence to be registered as lobbyists or foreign agents, as is required by the Department of Justice in the United States. Lobbying by the Japanese on legislators and bureaucrats is intense, but it is done privately. This policy invites criticism from the United States, who contends that Japanese policymaking is not transparent — meaning not out in the open — and therefore is undemocratic.

Many organizations also use pubic pressure, manipulate the press, organize demonstrations, hold conferences, and advocate their views in publications. It is in this public domain that the Japanese press plays its vital role. There are five national newspapers, ranging in circulation from 3 million to 8 million each, in addition to regional and local newspapers. The largest newspaper circulation in the United States is less than 2 million; the *Wall Street Journal* and *USA Today* are the only papers that come close to being national papers. In contrast, a typical Japanese household subscribes to one national, which delivers both morning and evening editions, and one local newspaper. In addition to several commercial networks, one national television network (NHK) transmits the same news from northern Hokkaido to southern Kagoshima. College professors, think-tank researchers, commentators, and reporters are often the guests of news talk shows on television. They also write extensively in weekly and monthly magazines and journals on trade issues and United States-Japan relations.

In both countries, domestic interest groups exert intense pressure on policymakers regarding trade issues. The process is democratic, reflecting different views of different interests. Political games are played intensively, creating complicated pull-and-push relationships.

What compounds this complexity is the role of the mass media, which transmits news from one country to another country almost instantly. The speed with which information reaches the other country has political implications that did not exist before high technology transformed newspapers and, later radio and television. In fact, trade negotiations today often proceed on two or three levels: actual negotiations between the two official delegations; semi-public consultations between groups of prominent leaders, often "wise men"; and political negotiations played out in the arena of pubic relations. Whoever presents a case more skillfully to the public often determines the perceptions of the trading partner's behavior. Perhaps this is the price democratic societies must pay to live with one another, but Japan has not performed well in this arena.

U.S. VERSUS JAPANESE STYLE OF NEGOTIATION

U.S. and Japanese approaches to trade issues are quite different. Since bilateral trade issues began to surface in the 1960s, a pattern has developed in which the Americans took the initiative in presenting their compliants, pressing for negotiations, and seeking specific solutions. Japan, still suffering from the inferiority complex instilled by its defeats in World War II and the occupation by the allies headed by the United States, often took a defensive and reactive posture. The pattern of concession at the sacrifice of domestic industries by Japan to U.S. demands was widely portrayed in the Japanese press, which fueled anti-American feelings. Although Japan had become a major power many Japanese policymakers particularly of the older generation, still acted as if their country was in the immediate post-war period. In the United States, disputes about particular goods were inflated by members of Congress when these goods were important in their districts, quickly making them national, not local, issues.

U.S. beef export is one example. Although the amount of beef exported from the United States to Japan was insignificant in overall trade, it became for the United States a symbol of a closed Japanese market under strict government controls. When beef imports were to be liberalized by Japan, U.S. beef exporters, who were guaranteed exports under a bilateral agreement that provided for quotas, might lose out to cheaper beef from Australia and South America. U.S. negotiators contended that so long as the principle of free trade was practiced, that would be acceptable.

Because the United States was a leading force in multilateral trade negotiations in the General Agreement on Tariffs and Trade, U.S. negotiators tended to use principles of free trade as a starting point, whereas the Japanese approach was often bogged down on specific issues.

Makoto Kuroda, formerly a senior MITI official and a key negotiator with the United States, observed that the Japanese do not set a specific objective in negotiation but are interested in reaching a practical level of compromise. In a dialogue with Glen Fukushima, a former USTR official and Kuroda's counterpart, Kuroda pointed out that the U.S. negotiators present the most desirable goal at first and will not be satisfied unless they get a perfect score. In contrast, the Japanese say no to the U.S. demands at first, measuring the U.S. reaction. Then, the Japanese present their proposal piecemeal, again measuring their counterpart's reaction at each step. Fukushima countered that because the U.S. objective is to have Japan lift trade barriers, demanding a 100 percent solution is necessary.[4]

Having studied Japanese negotiating style, U.S. negotiators tried a different approach during the SII talks, which was to appeal directly to the public in Japan. Deputy USTR S. Linn Williams was quoted in an interview as expressing satisfaction: "During the SII dialogue we found the feedback we received from the Japanese public to be very constructive." Some changes were being asked of Japanese people to agree with Washington on most points.[5] Whether that public sentiment will be reflected in Japanese policymakers' thinking is unclear. However, from the volatile domestic political situation and increasingly vocal consumers as voters, Japanese legislators and interest groups will probably not be able to ignore the public.

The perception of U.S. pressure produces two reactions in Japan. First is the resistance to such foreign pressure, or gai-atsu. The other is to use gai-atsu to achieve what is usually difficult to achieve if such pressure comes from domestic groups. Reactive responses and active use of gai-atsu have been familiar patterns in Japanese politics since modernization began in the nineteenth century. The United States has recently studied the political dynamics of Japan and begun to use this information to its own advantage.

The Japanese have long been known for their extensive use of the U.S. political system, particularly the practice of legal lobbying in Washington, D.C. As the relationship of interdependence deepens between the two countries so does the mutual use of domestic political tactics. This use can be possible only when both sides understand each other's complex political system. Many individuals in both countries advocate that a better understanding of each other's society and culture would surely lead to a better relationship. While this may be true, it may also be true that a better understanding could lead to the raw exploitation of each other's political vulnerabilities.

Recent trade negotiations between the United States and Japan have shown a marked change. Until recently, the two governments made a conscious effort to separate trade issues from other issues, particularly the security issue. Each time the Congress tried to link the two issues, the White House administration opposed such a move.

However, trade issues have begun to penetrate into security considerations as U.S. defense products have begun to rely more on Japanese-made parts. An agreement to produce jointly FSX, a new fighter plane, was worked out by the U.S. Defense and State Departments with the Japanese government but had to be rewritten. Too many objections came from the U.S. Commerce Department, which was backed by the Congress who feared that the Japanese were taking advantage of the agreement to acquire U.S. high technology.

Generally speaking, when specific products were an issue, the outcome of negotiations was also specific in numbers and percentages. If a certain industry was an issue, the goal could be gauged in specific deregulation or market share. But as the negotiations have moved from products to market to system, as with the SII talks, the criterion of specific numbers is no longer working.[6]

The SII agenda included a wide range of basic changes in both countries. Negotiators discussed not only abolishing or reforming Japan's Large Scale Retail Store Law to permit more U.S. businesses to operate in Japan, but they also discussed ways to improve the quality of education in the United States. Improving the quality of education should increase productivity.

Problems may arise in determining whether agreements reached under SII have been implemented. For instance, how can U.S. negotiators present the results of improved education to their Japanese counterparts? Do they use quantitative or qualitative data? If qualitative data is to be used, what is the philosophy by which quality of education is measured? How can a weak U.S. Department of Education impose such a policy because most budgets and administration in U.S. education are controlled by state and local governments?

While Japan's pledge in the SII talks to increase its public works projects can be measured by the amount of money spent, the U.S pledge to improve the quality of education may remain as a footnote. The declining quality of education in the United States, particularly in math and science at the precollege level, has serious implications in the quality of the work force. Corporations are already spending billions of dollars for remedial training in reading and math to improve the efficiency of their workers and quality control.

When asked how long it will take for the agreement to take effect, Williams cautioned, "three to five years, assuming that everything is done in the right order and at the right time." This statement also assumes that other factors do not interfere, such as exchange rate fluctuations, changes in interest rates, and so forth. The reduction of the U.S. federal deficit, another major item in the SII agreement, began to proceed before the Gulf War slowed normal government activity. Among the possible factors that could hamper the accomplishment of SII and other trade negotiations, the most drastic disruption is the Gulf War that began on January 16, 1991. (This is an assessment as of February 11, 1991.) Even so, the Bush Administration insists that expenditures on the war are manageable.

From the viewpoint of United States-Japan trade issues, the war contributed to changing the nature of the overall bilateral relationship. Before the war, U.S. criticism of Japan centered on trade issues. Japanese interest in the bilateral relationship also centered on trade. Although a trend to link trade with security has begun, that approach has been secondary so far.

When the multinational forces headed by the United States were engaged in war against Iraq, Japan's role in the war was pushed aside by trade issues, making them one of the issues, not *the* issue. However, what the United States perceived as Japan's behavior in trade issues has also cemented their image of Japan as an unwilling partner in a time of crisis.[7]

U.S. resentment in the past has turned into anger over what the United States perceived as Japan's unwillingness to contribute to the war effort. How such strong emotion might dictate the direction of future trade negotiations is uncertain. However, U.S. policymakers, particularly in the Congress, will harden their attitudes and will be less willing to change their image of Japan on specific issues.

In Japan, too, there is rising anti-U.S. sentiment at the grassroots level in response to criticism toward the Japanese by the United States. Before the Gulf War, the Japanese perceived that the United States had been pushing the Japanese around by demanding one thing after another. During the past four decades, the Japanese have been accustomed, and have been encouraged by the United States, to think of the world through the United States-Japan relationship.

When the Gulf War began and the Japanese government struggled to contribute to the multinational forces, the government was severely blocked by the public's strong opposition to sending self-defense forces (SDF) to the Middle East, even for noncombat missions. The government also failed to persuade both the pubic and opinion leaders that the war was international, not just a war between Saddam Hussein and George Bush. Because of this image, most comments, editorials, and letters of readers to newspapers reflect a mostly negative attitude toward a U.S. demand on Japanese contribution.

One factor that distorts the Japanese public's understanding of the war is an information vacuum. In most countries around the world, Cable News Network (CNN), the U.S. television station devoted entirely to news, is watched extensively. In contrast, only a small percentage of Japanese households subscribe to the satellite and cable network that transmits broadcasts from CNN.

Although Japanese correspondents are in the Middle East, the bulk of hard information about the war came from U.S. television news. Japanese networks broadcast only portions of such news with either Japanese superimposed or with simultaneous translation, the quality of which is not good. Japanese commentators often try to fill the vacuum by adding their interpretation to the news.

As a result, the Japanese public receives information through double and triple filters, which obscures the impact of the war. Because limited numbers of people have access to U.S. media and because of the language barrier, Japan is the only major power in the world not sharing the same information at the same speed and intensity with its allies.

Therefore, the Japanese public's interpretation of the war and arguments about the Japanese role in the war varied widely.[8] Opinions ranged from doing nothing, since Japan is incapable of taking active political leadership, to revising the Constitution to allow the SDF to dispatch forces to international conflicts. In the public opinion polls the majority agreed that Japan should contribute financially to multinational forces but were reluctant to send SDF personnel outside Japan.

Of the political parties, the ruling LDP pushed for contributing both financially and in manpower, but the Japan Socialist Party and the Japan Communist Party strongly opposed both types of contribution. The LDP used its majority in the House of Representatives to pass a package of laws that raises revenue from the issuance of special bonds and by increasing taxes on petroleum, tobacco, and corporate earnings to cover the $9 billion pledge to the multinational forces. But any tax or budget bill has to pass both houses, and the Japan Socialist Party and other opposition parties hold the majority in the upper house.

Former Prime Minister Toshiki Kaifu and senior leaders in the LDP saw the Gulf War as crucial to United States-Japan relations. Having been frustrated by the mounting trade issues with the United States, LDP leaders believe a crisis will occur if Japan does not come up with what the United States sees as a satisfactory contribution; bilateral relations will probably plunge further.

Nevertheless, the LDP leaders are finding it difficult to build a domestic political coalition to support their objective. This is the first time since 1945 that Japan has faced a test of the assumption in the Constitution that expresses a desire for peace, and that international trust alone shall guarantee peace. The assumption has shielded the Japanese from questioning its validity for four decades.

When the Gulf War ended, United States-Japan relations were pushed into sharply focused questions of the workability of the alliance. It is quite possible that trade issues, both existing and future, might not escape the politicized atmosphere in which the issue is not trade but commitment to the alliance itself. Perhaps the Gulf War was the first opportunity for Japan to emerge from its post-war insularity.

RECOMMENDATIONS FOR IMPROVED UNITED STATES-JAPAN RELATIONS

Aside from the current pressing matters, what can be done to guide United States-Japan relations on a constructive path? As the shift in focus of the trade issues indicates, we have entered an era of testing values and ways of thinking. Because the human mind shapes values, intense human exchange and interaction is the prerequisite to the future relationship.

In tourism, art, and education, the exchange between the two countries has reached a substantial level. In business, slowly but steadily, Japan and the United States have begun to work side by side in each other's country. Perhaps the time has come to extend the exchange into government and legislative bodies.

Several Japanese legislators have already hired U.S. citizens to their staffs in Tokyo. Those U.S. citizens are young, majored in Japanese studies and are fluent in Japanese. In Washington, too, young Japanese, mostly graduate students, have worked in the offices of congressmen and on committees. But the exchange is experi-mental and small scale and should be expanded.

Opportunities should exist for U.S. citizens to work in Japanese ministries and for Japanese to work in U.S. government agencies as interns. Those interns could develop their own network so that they could exchange observations about the country in which they worked, do comparative studies, and publish their work.

Existing exchange programs between members of the U.S. Congress and the National Diet should also be expanded. Japan should pass a law on foreign agent registration that enables U.S. lobbyists to be legally and openly agents for their clients in Japan, operating within the Japanese political system. In the United States, there should be a ceiling or restriction on the number of political appointments in the administration so that each department could promote inside experts with fluency in regional languages. This policy would attract those who have invested substantial time in their careers concentrating on specific countries, such as Japan, for government services.

Concurrently, more political appointments should be made in Japanese ministries to provide a broader and more global dimension to bureaucratic thinking. Examples of such appointments have already occurred, particularly in the foreign service, whereby invited officials of other ministries and experts from academia and journalism assume senior diplomatic posts. Such practice should be expanded to other ministries.

In summary, the proposal here is an intense exchange of minds both within each country and between the two countries. This may be the most difficult aspect in any bilateral relationship in which cultural differences are wide and deep. But the United States and Japan have reached this stage. If both sides are interested in keeping their alliance, they should start working on it.

NOTES

1. For economic, political, and ideological aspects of United States-Japan trade issues, see a continuing series of articles by Glen S. Fukushima in *Asahi Journal Weekly* (starting January 4, 1991), Tokyo, entitled "Nichibei Keizai Masatsu No Seijigaku" (Politics of United States-Japan Economic Conflicts). Fukushima is former Deputy Assistant USTR for Japan and China and is currently director, Public Policy and Business Development, AT&T Japan Ltd. in Tokyo.

For how the U.S. administration, Congress, and interest groups deal with each other on economic and international trade issues, see *Dollar Politics: Exchange Rate Policymaking in the United States*, by I. M. Destler and C. Randall Henning, Institute for International Economics, Washington, D.C., 1989. This is a study about the effect of exchange rate policy on U.S. business and employment during the 1980s, which in turn politicized monetary and trade policymaking by the Reagan Administration.

2. *How the Liberal Democrats Rule Japan* by Nathaniel Thayer (Princeton University Press, 1969) is an authoritative study on the Japanese political system focusing on how the ruling party came to power and continues to hold office.

3. To understand how committee membership in the Japanese Diet functions for each faction and individual members, see *Zoku Giin No Kenkyu* (A Study on the Tribe Members in the National Diet) by Takashi Inoguchi and Tomoaki Iwai, *Nihon Keizai Shimbun-sha* (Japan Economic Journal), Tokyo, 1987. This is a detailed study about Japanese parliamentarians who sit on key committees in the Diet, their factions, and their power relationships with industries they oversee. Members of each committee are called tribe members, such as construction tribe and postal and telecommunication tribe.

On the postal and telecommunication tribe, the authors conclude that the relationship between the Ministry of Postal and Telecomunications (MPT) and the tribe members is perhaps the closest, as their mutual interest is totally compatible. MPT's authority to grant licenses in the information and telecommunication industry is used for political campaigns. As the industry reaps enormous profit from licensing, membership on the postal and telecommunication tribe is one of the choicest for Diet members. Members of the powerful faction led by former Prime Minister Kakuei Tanaka hold more than half the membership.

However, with the rapid move toward deregulation, turf battles between the MPT and other ministries has been intensifying. MITI and MPT/postal and telecommunication tribes are competing for control of the computer industry. The Ministries of Construction, Transportation, Finance, and Agriculture are also trying to get administrative control in the information and telecommunications industries.

4. See *Nihon Keizai Shim-bun* (Japan Economic Journal), "Sunday Nikkei Debate" between Makoto Kuroda and Glen S. Fukushima, Tokyo, December 9, 1990 (in Japanese).

5. See *Japan Economic Survey*, Commentary Section, Japan Economic Institute, Washington, D.C., January 1990.

6. To examine various characteristics of Japanese business, such as keiretsu and Japanese investment in the United States, and how such characteristics may be transformed by the negotiations on the SII, see *Kozo Chosei: Nihon Kiqyo Ni Nani Ga Dekiruka* (Structural Adjustment: What Can Japanese Corporations Do?), Niho Keizai Shimbun-sha, Tokyo, 1990. A group of Nihon Keizai reporters reviewed issues that were raised during the SII talks.

7. See *JEI Report*, No. 5A, Washington, D.C., Japan Economic Institute, February 8, 1991, entitled "The 102nd Congress and Japan: An Outlook," by Margo Grim. This is a detailed analysis of the mood in the U.S. Congress on United States-Japan relations after the Gulf War began: an overview of past trade legislation, the balance of party power in the Congress, and the composition of House and Senate committee chairmanship relating to United States-Japan relations.

8. For the diversity of public opinion in Japan on the Gulf War, see *Asahi Shimbun*, January 26, 1991 (14th edition, p. 31) with the headline, "A Heavy Choice on War and Peace," and interviews on the streets in Tokyo, Osaka, Nagoya, and Fukuoka. Most of those interviewed opposed sending self-defense force personnel to the Gulf and were even reluctant to have Japan make a financial contribution.

However, another newspaper, *Sankei Shimbun*, interviewed 200 government officials and business executives in Tokyo to illustrate a gap in thinking between those in policymaking positions and the public. The interviews took place after Iraq's invasions of Kuwait on August 2, 1990, but before the multinational forces' attack on Iraq and Kuwait on January 16, 1991. The result of the interviews was published on January 3, 1991. Most officials from 23 ministries in the central government and business executives from 74 corporations in the first section of the Tokyo Stock Exchange list were at "kacho" (director) level in middle-management positions.

Among them, 65 percent of the government officials and 76 percent of the business executives were of the opinion that Japan should go beyond merely being an economic power to exercise political leadership in general. Among the government officials, 42 percent supported the idea of military action against Iraq if Iraq did not comply with the UN resolutions calling for Iraqi troop withdrawal from Kuwait. In contrast, 71 percent of the business executives favored peaceful solutions through diplomatic negotiations (before the January 16, 1991, attack).

On sending SDF personnel to the Gulf, half of the business executives wanted them to be only on noncombat missions, but 56 percent of the government officials supported direct military cooperation or participation in the UN peace preservations forces. There was growing concern about Japan's weak intelligence-gathering capability in times of crises, the Gulf Crisis being one example. Among the government officials, 17 percent supported the idea of establishing an information agency similar to the Central Intelligence Agency in the United States, as did 23 percent of the business executives.

A new twist in opinion about Japan's foreign policy in the survey was that although most government officials still considered United States-Japan relations and the security alliance to be the most important, 55 percent of the business executives supported the idea of reconsidering that basic policy, urging Japan to take a stand independent of the United States-Japan alliance.

4

Japan's International Trade in Telecommunications Services

Hajime Oniki

Japan's telecommunication industry was liberalized in 1985. Before the liberalization, Nippon Telephone and Telegraph (NTT) was the state-owned monopoly. In April 1985, competition was introduced by privatizing NTT and allowing three new common carriers (NCCs) to operate nationwide. International telecommunication in Japan became competitive in October 1989, when two new international common carriers began operating.

The 1985 Telecommunication Business Law of Japan recognizes two categories of carriers: type I and type II. Type I carriers operate with transmission circuits, while type II carriers do not. Although telecommunications business by type I carriers is heavily regulated by the Ministry of Post and Telecommunications (MPT), business by type II carriers was almost completely liberalized in April 1985. In particular, telecommunications service trade is free in Japan. However, many barriers still exist for foreigners to conduct telecommunications business in Japan.

This chapter summarizes business and economic realities in Japan's telecommunications industry and telecommunications service trade. The discussion will focus on implications of the liberalization of Japan's telecommunications industry. I will try to consider the background business conditions of Japan's telecommunication industry and the current international environment of Japan's telecommunication industry in quite different ways. Some conditions work in the short run and others in the long run: Consequences arising from economic structures can be changed little, and phenomena coming from political activities may somehow be controlled.

The arguments in this chapter are:

The domestic production of enhanced services in Japan has come near to the stage of takeoff.

International trade of telecommunications services is still in its infancy in Japan, for both demand and the provider.

The United States and Western European countries have a comparative advantage of producing and exporting telecommunications services over Japan. There seems to be little possibility for Japan to catch up within a few years.

Liberalization of Japan's telecommunications industry and telecommunications service trade in 1985 encouraged domestic networking but not Japan's importation of telecommunications services from abroad, even though Japan did not have comparative advantage in telecommunications services. The main reason for this was the presence of language and sociocultural barriers to importing telecommunications services from abroad, for domestic production of telecommunications services from abroad, and for domestic networking.

Massive trade in telecommunications services, import or export, is not possible in the near future, because the barrier will not go away soon. Exceptions are the import of information by specialists (academic, financial, etc.), information flows for network-oriented companies (airlines and others), and Japan's export of telecommunications services to branches of Japanese companies established abroad.

In the long run, however, once flexible and user-friendly telecommunications services become available on, for example, artificial intelligence technology, the barriers will be overcome and international trade of telecommunications services may start growing rapidly.

First, I will consider the technological, economic, and political background of Japan's telecommunications industry. Next, current activities in telecommunications services will be described, and policymaking by the Japanese government will be discussed. Finally, the liberalization of Japan's telecommunications industry will be evaluated, and a brief forecast of the industry in the near future will be given.

JAPAN'S TELECOMMUNICATIONS INDUSTRY

Technology

The development of information and communication technology in Japan began in the early 1970s. Japan now leads the world in manufacturing large-scale integrated (LSI) memories, small and personal computers, and other peripherals. However, the Japanese strength of producing information products lies more in hardware than in software or systems. The same is true with Japan's telecommunications industry. Japanese telecommunications technology is advanced in the quality of terminals, circuits, and switching machines. The range and quality of its services, however, is less advanced. For example, people who travel to Japan will see that virtually every coin (and card) telephone on the street is working. When placing a call, whether at home or in a street, there is little chance that one gets an incomplete or poor connection. A call is either connected well or not connected because the line is busy. Old style telephone terminals could last for decades without service. After terminal sale was liberalized in Japan, I purchased a shiny new model that looked intelligent. I was then left with an old NTT terminal, which seemed to have no value. For the purpose of an experiment, I tried to break the old terminal by pulling the power cord and also by throwing the instrument on the floor. To my surprise, the cord did not come out from a casual pull, and the terminal still worked after being dropped on the floor. The hardware was firmly designed and manufactured. This shows that NTT put great emphasis on the quality of its hardware.

Today, telecommunications network technology depends heavily on software. We know that even the basic service, that is, handling public telephone calls, is done by software with digital switching machines. The importance of software is greater in producing enhanced services such as digital data transmission, message switching and storing, and electronic mail. Today the quality of telecommunications services is largely determined by the quality of the software supporting them. Furthermore, the services of information providers, such as data bases or videotexts, are nothing but services of the software that these providers use.

The development of technology for telecommunications service production has been slow in Japan. Some evidence of this is that, first, an academic computer network linking 7 major universities in Japan was started only 10 years ago, more than 10 years behind the United States' ARPANET. A universal network for all Japanese universities is yet to be constructed. Consequently, electronic mail in the Japanese language is available to university scholars but is not used widely. Second, the electric connection of personal computers to the telephone network was permitted only a few years ago, at about the same time that Japan's telecommunications industry was liberalized. Before that time, only acoustic connection was allowed. For this reason, the price of modems in Japan used to be several times higher than their world price because of a lack of demand. Today the price of modems is at the world-price level.

The technological difference between the United States and Japan in telecommunications service production is somewhere between 5 and 10 years. The existence of such a large gap, however, may not be explained by technological factors alone The lack of demand for sophisticated telecommunications services from the Japanese users and the limitation imposed by the Japanese language, which uses thousands of characters for daily communication, may also be responsible.

The situation is changing rapidly now, at least as far as demand. Today, Japanese users complain that the variety of services provided by NTT is less than that available in U.S. corporations, and banks rely on electronic data transmission for intra- and interfirm information exchanges. Youngsters capable of using personal computers are turning from game playing to networking. The Ministry of Education of Japan established a new institution responsible for constructing a nationwide academic computer network. In Japan, computers that were once used as stand-alone machines are finally being connected through telephone circuits, local-area networks (LANs), and wide-area networks (WANs). Integrated Services Digital Network (ISDN) services, which was started by NTT 18 months ago, will accelerate this movement. However, it will probably take at least a few more years, perhaps longer, for Japan to reach the level of networking services presently available in the United States and Western European countries.

Economy

Comparative Advantage or Disadvantage of Producing Telecommunications Services

The advantage of producing and exporting goods and services depends on the cost at which goods or services are produced. What determines a country's pattern of trade is not the absolute level of the cost relative to that at which the goods or the services are produced in foreign countries. This is called "the theory of comparative advantage of production and trade." According to this theory, it is impossible for a single country, whether developed or underdeveloped, to have an advantage in production and trade of every commodity and every service. If a country has comparative advantage in some goods, it must have comparative disadvantage in some others. The goods or services in which a country has comparative advantage can be exported abroad.

The principle of comparative advantage, however, determines the pattern of trade only in the long run. In the short run, other factors are more important. They are macroeconomic conditions, trade and transactions costs, tariffs and government regulations, and social and political barriers to trade.

Japan does not have comparative advantage in producing telecommunications services, relative to the United States or Western European countries. This fact is not expected to change for at least a few years. Therefore, little possibility exists for Japan to export telecommunications services to the United States or for Western European countries to extend their telecommunications services to Japan, at least not in the short run. Factors other than comparative advantage prevent Japan from importing telecommunications services from the United States or Western European countries, except in special cases.

Macroeconomic Conditions

Macroeconomic conditions in Japan influence telecommunications service trade through two routes: by driving the export of telecommunications service trade from Japan and by amplifying political activities, demanding Japan to lower import barriers and to increase the import of goods and services, including telecommunications services.

International macroeconomic conditions in Japan are characterized by its huge trade surplus since the beginning of the 1980s. The economic cause of the trade surplus is that Japan consumes less and saves more relative to other countries, especially relative to the United States. Japan is like an individual who works hard and earns a lot, but does not spend as much as he earns and, thus, is left with a large amount of extra money that becomes his savings. When an individual has extra money, he deposits it at a bank or buys securities or stocks. When a country has extra money, it can buy foreign securities or stocks, as Japan is doing now. Unlike an individual, however, a country with extra money cannot go to a bank to make a deposit. A country "saves" by acquiring foreign securities or stocks in exchange for goods and services. Why the propensity to save is high in Japan relative to the United States and other advanced countries has been discussed repeatedly by economists and policymakers.

The trade imbalance affects telecommunications service trade in two ways. First, the presence of a large amount of Japan's savings to be deposited abroad means an increase in the export of telecommunications service trade from Japan. Nevertheless, Japan's comparative disadvantage in producing telecommuncations services is so large that few are exported from Japan. Second, Japan's trade imbalance affects telecommunications service trade through political activities. Barriers to import, if defined broadly, certainly exist in Japan now. Whether the barriers play a significant role in forming Japan's trade imbalance is debatable. I believe that even if the trade barriers were removed completely, Japan's trade imbalance would still remain large, because the Japanese work force would still save a lot and would not spend much on consuming imported goods, except on a few items like beef, oranges, and rice. From the viewpoint of the United States, especially from the viewpoint of the U.S. Congress, Japan's trade imbalance looks like a direct consequence of these trade barriers. The U.S. government, standing on the thesis of free trade, considers the barriers to be undesirable, and thus, they should be removed as soon as possible. In addition, in bilateral trade negotiations with Japan, the United States strategically chooses target commodities for which the barriers are to be removed. Telecommunications services have become one such target.

International Relations

Multilateral Relations

The General Agreement of Tariffs and Trade (GATT) ministerial meeting in September 1986 started the new Uruguay Round. Service trade has been discussed in the GATT Group of negotiations on Service (GNS) since then. Further, the Trade Negotiations Committee meeting at the ministerial level in Montreal, Canada, held on December 9, 1988, adopted a Statement of Trade in Services.[1] In recent GNS meetings, the tradability of telecommunications services, except basic telephony, is widely endorsed. However, the definition of items for trade, in relation to the International Telecommunications Union, equipment trade, and others, are yet to be resolved. The international political world wants the successful outcome of the Uruguay Round, despite the opposition by developing countries, and the possibility of having a second Uruguay Round is foreseen.[2]

The Information Computer and Communication Policy of the organization for Economic Cooperation and Development (OECD) conducted a comprehensive study on the possibility of developing telecommunications service trade, which is called telecommunication network-based services in the report. Institutional provision of telecommunications service trade in OECD member countries are surveyed and summarized.[3]

The Commission for European Community is attempting to form a consistent set of telecommunications policies by combining regulation and liberalization by European Community (EC) countries, so that a single European market for telecommunications services may be established by 1992. Full competition for the provision of all services except basic telephony is foreseen. Some important objectives of the commission are: equilibrium service charges for data transmission, harmonization for technical access to pubic networks, cost-oriented tariff structures, leased circuits to be interconnected with shared use and resale, and liberalized satellite usage.[4]

Bilateral Relation with the United States

The view of the U.S. government on future courses of information and telecommunications may be seen in a recent report from the National Telecommunications and Information Administration (NTIA), in which it is stressed that, on recognizing challenges for the coming information age the United States should maintain technological and economic leadership in the world.[5]

The recent trade policy of the U.S. government is characterized by an emphasis placed on bilateral trade negotiations. The Canada-United States Free Trade Agreement began successfully in January 1989. A major component of the U.S. trade policy with Japan has been to promote negotiations to open Japanese markets for certain goods or services. Because Japan exports large amounts of manufactured goods to the United States, possible retaliation by imposing restrictions on Japanese exports to the United States is used as leverage by the U.S. government. Telecommunications services are regarded as one of the targets strategically chosen for United States-Japan trade negotiations.

TELECOMMUNICATIONS SERVICES IN JAPAN

Telecommunications Industry in the Japanese Economy

From direct observations, we believe that the production of Japan's telecommunications services, both basic and enhanced, has grown rapidly since the 1985 liberalization. Yet, statistical data are not available to confirm this directly.

Liberalization of Japan's Telecommunications Industry

Before the 1985 liberalization, NTT was the state-owned common carrier operating as a monopoly for domestic telecommunications. Kokusai Denshin Denwa (KDD), the international telephone corporation created as a private corporation in 1952, was the monopoly common carrier for international telecommunications. In April 1985, competition was introduced by privatizing NTT and allowing three domestic NCCs to operate nationwide and other carriers to operate regionally or with mobile phones. International telecommunications in Japan became competitive in October 1989 when two new international common carriers began operating.

Of the two categories of carriers recognized by the 1985 Telecommunication Business Law of Japan, type I carriers operate with transmission circuits, type II carriers without. Type II carriers are regulated by the MPT in their entry/exit, pricing, service provision, and so on. Foreign owners are allowed to acquire a maximum of one-third of the shares of a type I carrier. Now, there are 17 domestic type I carriers, including NTT, and 3 international type I carriers, including KDD. NTT and KDD are established by the NTT Organization Law and the KDD Organization Law, respectively. They are both regulated by MPT more heavily than other type I carriers.

Telecommunications business by type II carriers was almost completely liberalized in April 1985; in particular, telecommunications service trade, import or export, is free in Japan. Foreign ownership of a type II carrier is fully allowed. There is free entry to the industry and no restriction on pricing or operations, including resale of leased circuits.

The Telecommunication Business Law defines two subcategories of type II carriers: general type II carriers and special type II carriers. Special type II carriers are those operating with 500 or more circuits (measured in terms of the unit equivalent to 1,200 bits/second capacity) or those operating internationally. A slight difference exists between general type II carriers and special type II carriers in entering the industry. General type II carriers need only to report their entry to MPT; special type II carriers need to register themselves with MPT. MPT may reject application for special type II carriership when applicants are judged not qualified according to the criterion given by the law. All in all, however, this difference is small, and we can consider that business by type II carriers is almost completely liberalized. Since 1985 more than 300 type II carriers have been established, including 7 special type II carriers who operate internationally.

MPT's regulation of Japan's telecommunications industry is based on the distinction of type I and type II carriers, which is done using a facility-based definition. This contrasts with the regulation of carriers in the United States, in which the concept of basic and enhanced services are used. It may be called a functional definition. In GNS meetings of the GATT Uruguay Round, the functional definition of telecommunications business has become more popular. It is therefore expected that the Japanese definition based on circuit ownership will soon have to be revised.

According to a 1989 OECD study on telecommunications network-based services, Japan is one of the three countries allowing free resale of leased circuits; the other two countries are Germany and the United States.[6] Thus, we may state that, at least in the institutional provision, Japan is one of the most liberalized countries in the telecommunications business, except with regard to the basic service — conventional telephony. We may argue, however, that many barriers still exist for foreigners to conduct telecommunication business in Japan.

On October 1, 1989, the Telecommunications Policy Committee, responsible for drawing major policy plans for Japan's telecommunications industry, filed an interim report with MPT. The 1985 NTT Organization Law states that the law should be reviewed and revised by the end of the 1990 Japanese fiscal year. The report has suggested that NTT may have to be divided into two or more companies to facilitate competition. Three alternative plans are suggested: dividing NTT into one long-distance carrier and one nationwide company for local operations, dividing NTT into one long-distance carrier and a number of regional companies, and dividing NTT into several regional companies operating as long-distance and local carriers. The leaders and workers union of NTT, and many of the electronic manufacturers that used to be within the NTT family, expressed opposition to the report. The proposal is favored, naturally, by all three NCCs. It seems that the majority of opinions are not in favor of the report because of the large cost of dividing NTT.

Demand for Telecommunications Services in Japan

To describe the current situation of production and trade of telecommunications services in Japan, four groups of (potential) users are identified: professional users, network-oriented companies, households and consumers, and other companies.

Professionals who need to use telecommunications services beyond the basic service are academics, lawyers, medical doctors, financial specialists, and others. Users in this group need to access a particular source of information for conducting their professional activities. Accessing data bases, exchanging electronic mail, performing data collection, and having remote control are typical examples.

Thus, the demand for telecommunications services by professionals arises from their demand for specialized information and specialized informational activities. In such a case, the price of telecommunications services is not an important factor. Rather, the demand is determined by the quality of telecommunications services and by the quality of information services from which the demand for telecommunications services is generated. In terms of economic theory, the demand for telecommunications services from professional users is price inelastic but quality elastic.

In Japan, access to data bases and data banks in the United States started approximately 10 years ago. Initially, international public telephone networks were used, and the price was prohibitively high. KDD then provided a packet exchange service to let users connect their computer terminals in Japan with mainframes in the United

States. The price of this service was still high under the monopoly of KDD. Recently, however, some special type II carriers started providing computer access service jointly with U.S. gateway services providers, such as TELENET and TYMNET. The price has come down significantly because of competition.

The demand for telecommunications services by professional users seems to be growing steadily, although no data are available. Services provided by foreign gateway providers and foreign data base operators are part of the import of telecommunications services to Japan. The amount of this import should not be negligible. Government regulation in this category of telecommunications services, however, may not be as effective as in other categories because professionals will get what they need to get at any price.

The second group of users — network-oriented companies — are typically airline and railroad companies, travel agents, hotel networks, financial investors, banks, and insurance companies. Telecommunications is not only needed but is vital for users in this group. Today, airline or railroad companies cannot operate without telecommunications. For this reason, the demand for telecommunications services from users in this group is quality elastic. The demand is price inelastic if users cannot find an alternative carrier, as when the carrier has a domestic monopoly. The demand will be highly price elastic, if the company operates internationally, since it can choose desirable services from multiple sources.

Hong Kong and Singapore are two Asian newly industrialized economies having exploited the benefit of providing efficient telecommunications network services since the middle of the 1970s. Japan is a latecomer in this regard, since networking developed slowly in Japan. During recent years, however, the demand for telecommunications services from network-oriented companies grew rapidly in Japan, mainly because the nation has become the largest supplier of financial capital in the world, generating a large demand for telecommunications services.

The groups of professional users and network-oriented companies are a firm source of the demand for telecommunications network services. However, the size of these groups relative to the whole society is small. Revenues that telecommunications carriers can get from these groups, therefore, cannot be as large as revenues from old telephony.

The third group of users of telecommunications services is households and consumers. In Japan, the demand for telecommunications services from this group is still insignificant. Only two types of activities, although minor, may be noted. One is stock trading by means of a game machine, equipped with an inexpensive modem. The other is personal computer (PC) communication, which is done by hooking up a PC to some mainframe through conventional telephone network. Videotexts, like French MINITEL, are not yet popular in Japan. Daily activities by consumers, such as banking or shopping, may be done electronically in the near future, perhaps by using game machines or touch-tone telephone terminals with some intelligence attached, but it is not a current issue.

Finally, consider the fourth group of users of telecommunications services, companies other than network-oriented companies. In Japan, as well as in the United States or Western European countries, networking has become important for these companies to grow and to save costs. Expansion of the market in which companies sell their products or services has made it more advantageous for them to access to their customers electronically. Electronic exchange of data for ordering, shipping, billing, and paying has become a more efficient means than relying on human services.

Electronic data interchange (EDI) is becoming popular in Japan among these companies. Since facsimiles were introduced widely in Japan, some EDI was done by means of facsimile transmission. In 1988 and 1989, the need for EDI was recognized widely: seminars are being held for promoting EDI. Some large trading companies developed their own protocols for EDI and tried to enclose their customers by connecting them to their EDI system. This effort, however, was unsuccessful.

Today, Japan is in the process of establishing business protocols for EDI. Banks and insurance companies have already established their protocols. Retail and wholesale companies, manufacturing companies, and construction companies are trying to follow. The need for a general business protocol for each industry was recognized only recently. Standardized protocols should become popular within a few years, and systematic development of EDI in many industries will be seen thereafter. One expert in EDI estimated that Japan was five years behind the United States and Western European countries in developing EDI in manufacturing and service industries.

Liberalization of Japan's Telecommunications Industry and Telecommunications Service Trade

What then were the effects of the 1985 liberalization of Japan's telecommunications industry on current telecommunications service trade in Japan? The liberalization of the basic service lowered its price, contributing to the growth of the telecommunications industry. This trend is expected to continue for a few years in domestic and international telecommunications business.

With regard to the demand for enhanced telecommunications services arising from the first two groups of users, that is, professional users and network-oriented companies, the liberalization of enhanced services worked favorably to Japanese users, to Japanese providers of the basic service, and to foreign providers of enhanced services. The only loser in the short run was KDD.

Regarding users in the last group — companies other than network-oriented ones — it is remarkable that no importation from foreign service providers is observed, even though the United States and Western European countries are a few years ahead of Japan in EDI, Japan's telecommunications service market is completely liberalized, and EDI is badly needed by Japanese companies now. The presence of language and other sociocultural "barriers" to importing EDI services from abroad is possibly a factor.

In the United States and Western European countries, EDI systems are developed in the English language; human services, needed for education, training, and maintenance, which are indispensable for effective use of the systems, are supplied in the English language. In Japan, such systems may be acceptable by specialists or companies operating internationally, but they are not acceptable by most ordinary companies. For workers in these ordinary companies who are not experts in EDI, EDI would not be usable without careful orientation and follow-up support, which could only be done in the native language, Japanese. For this reason, importing foreign EDI to Japan does not pay. It would be too costly for a foreign service provider to supply its EDI services in the Japanese language. It might be possible if a large amount of money had been invested to convert a U.S. or European EDI system into one that fit into the Japanese business environment. Such a large-scale project could beat small-scale domestic EDI operations. The amount of money needed for this might be too large, and the risk factor might not be neglected.

Thus, the liberalization of Japan's telecommunications industry did not bring foreign services to one of the most promising markets of telecommunications services in Japan. The liberalization worked favorably for the production of domestic telecommunications services, because the liberalization brought information and stimulus for the development of networking.

There is a difference between liberalization of a merchandise market and liberalization of a service market. Merchandise is homogeneous and does not need training and maintenance as much as a service market does. Therefore, merchandise can penetrate into foreign markets much easier than services can. In other words, transaction costs of service trade are much higher than those for merchandise trade.

Although no statistics are available, the exportation of telecommunications services by Japanese special type II carriers are believed to be increasing steadily. The demand comes form a large number of branches of Japanese companies operating abroad. In the past, exchanging information between a headquarters in Japan and foreign branches was done by facsimile. Now electronic data transmission is cheaper and more efficient. Japanese special type II carriers have an advantage over foreign providers in assisting them, although the same must be true for foreign telecommunications providers who are assisting foreign companies operating in Japan.

Policymaking by MPT

Judging by what was observed in the past, we can state that MPT's policy is formed on three elements: promotion of free competition in the domestic and international telecommunication markets, consideration of political and economic relations with the United States, and protection of Japanese incumbent firms in the domestic market.

It is impossible to write a policy satisfying these three elements. The question then arises as to what principle MPT uses in forming a decision, and, if reconciliation is done, what weight MPT places on each of the three elements in forming a policy. It seems that the long-term trend in MPT's policy formation is to emphasize the thesis of free trade of telecommunications services. In the short term, however, MPT's decision seems to be sensitive to politics and other factors. It seems impossible to predict what policy MPT will adopt on a particular occasion. Three cases are presented here to explain why:

Case 1: MPT has given an unexpectedly large number (17 by 1989) of type I licenses since the 1985 liberalization of the telecommunications market.

Case 2: When Japan's Telecommunication Business Law was being prepared by MPT, it was planned that the special type II carriers would be regulated by MPT more strongly than they are now. In particular, entry into the industry as a special type II carrier was to be *permitted* by MPT. This plan was criticized by the U.S. Trade Representative on the ground that a need for MPT's permission for entry by a special type II carrier would be a barrier to foreign providers operating in Japan. The Ministry of International Trade and Industry also criticized the plan because they feared possible retaliation by the United States on the Japanese exportation of manufactured goods to the United States. MPT eventually conceded, and the draft of the law was rewritten so that a special type II carrier needs only to register itself with MPT.

Case 3: In may 1989, Motorola, Inc., of America demanded from MPT that the Daini Denden, one of the Japanese NCCs having decided to use Motorola's handy portable telephone terminal, be given permission to operate in the Tokyo area as well as in the Kansai area. MPT was planning to give a license to the Daini Denden to operate in the Kansai and other areas of Japan, but not in the Tokyo area, which was considered by far the largest market in Japan. MPT opposed this demand on the grounds that no more bandwidth was available for additional allocation to the Daini Denden in the Tokyo area. After some exchange on technical points about available bandwidth and some interchange by higher political figures, MPT agreed to let NTT and the Daini Denden share a certain bandwidth so that Motorola's terminals could be used in the Tokyo area.

In these three cases, MPT's decision was criticized in Japan both by protectionists and by free-trade supporters. We can see that MPT made a number of attempts to protect Japanese carriers and tried not to open Japanese markets. Regarding competition in the domestic market, MPT tends to promote competition rather than to limit it.

CONCLUSION

In this chapter, we have seen that the liberalization of Japan's telecommunications industry was effective for bringing in competition in the basic service market. The future organization of the industry is uncertain because the question of reorganizing NTT is not yet settled. We have also seen that with the level of technology available today, international trade of enhanced services at a rate comparable with that of merchandise trade is unlikely. However, because telecommunications technology is rapidly advancing, we do not know how long this trend will continue. If, for example, flexible and user-friendly telecommunications services are developed with artificial intelligence language and other barriers may be overcome so that telecommunications service trade may become popular worldwide. What we know is that we only stand at the entrance to a world in which advanced information and telecommunications technology may give us a wide range of activities much greater than we can now contemplate.

NOTES

1. "Montreal Ministerial Statement on Trade in Services," Transnational Data and Communications Report, Vol. XII, No. 5, 1989.

2. Russell Pipe, Transnational Data and Communications, personnal communication.

3. OECD. Telecommunication Network-Based Services: Policy Implications, Information Computer Communications Policy 18. Paris: OECD, 1989.

4. Commission of the European Communities. "Towards a Dynamic European Community: Green Paper on the Development of the Common Market for Telecommunications Services and Equipment." Brussels: CEC, 1987.

5. National Telecommunications and Information Administration. *NTIA Telecom 2000*. Washington, DC: U.S. Department of Commerce, 1988.

6. OECD, 1988.

REFERENCES

Bureau of Economic Analysis. *Survey of Current Business*, Vol. 69, No. 3, p. 32. Washington, DC: U.S. Department of Commerce, 1989.

"Corporate Users and KDD — Japanese Telecommunications," Transnational Data and Communications Report, Vol. XII, No. 3, 1989.

Peterson, J. "Towards a Taxonomy of New Telecommunication Services," Discussion paper, Brunei University, 1989.

"Telecom Services face Trade Negotiations — GNS Accelerates Work," Transnational Data and Communications Report, Vol. XII, No. 3, 1989.

"Telecom Services Considered for Trade Regime — Caution Recommended," Transnational Data and Communications Report, Vol. XII, No. 5, 1989.

5

GATT, the Telecom Annex, and Telecommunications Trade: The Good, the Bad, and the Ugly

Jonathan Aronson

During the Uruguay Round of the General Agreement on Tariffs and Trade (GATT) negotiations, a telecommunications annex was proposed as part of the framework agreement for trade in services to rewrite the "rules of the game" for international trade in telecommunications services. Unfortunately, this annex contributed to the failure of the GATT negotiations, even though disagreement over agricultural issues was the chief cause.

This chapter examines the evolution of the controversy over the issue of trade in telecommunications services. It attempts to put United States-Japan telecommunications services and the telecommunications annex into perspective.

THE GOOD

Telecommunications services in the trade context have been embedded in the broader and more far reaching trade in services. Hence, we should look at how trade in services emerged as an issue, because the original GATT articles have nothing to do with services. The only service mentioned in the GATT articles is the movie industry — Articles 3 and 4. No other services are mentioned, and indeed there was no intention to mention other services. In the 1940s, services were not considered to be tradable goods. The prevailing thought was that services, including telecommunications services, could not be traded as they were jointly provided. For example, if the United States and Japan are sending information back and forth, either by cable or satellite, somewhere in mid-ocean there is a hand-off between AT&T and KDD. Up to mid-ocean, service is provided by

AT&T and after that it is provided by KDD. The companies settle accounts between themselves, much like the U.S. Post Office.

Trade in services was raised as an issue by Hugh Corbett, an Australian journalist for the *Financial Times* in the mid-1960s. He began advocating the importance of services in the world economy. Nonetheless, as neither he nor anyone else introduced a specific rationale for its importance, trade in services continued to be ignored.

In 1979, the United States persuaded members of the Organization for Economic Cooperation and Development (OECD) to undertake a study of trade in services. The study found that services are actually a key part of the world economy and, thus, deserved attention. Meanwhile, the United States began to get interested and a few companies including the American International Group (an insurance company) and American Express began to notice that nowhere in U.S. trade legislation was the word services used. Their influence resulted in the term "trade in goods and services" being included in the Trade Act of 1974. Senator Daniel Inouye of Hawaii was one of the early leaders of a small band of people who wanted to put services on the agenda. This group was called the friends of services by those in government or more simply the "services Mafia."

During the Tokyo Round of the GATT negotiations in the 1970s, the United States proposed the negotiation of a trade in services agreement. This proposal was withdrawn by U.S. trade negotiator Robert Strauss because European countries failed to support the proposal on the basis that neither they nor the United States understood enough about the subject to pursue it at that time. However, Robert Strauss promised U.S. service providers that services would be a priority at the next round of GATT talks.

The Tokyo Round ended in 1979. Shortly thereafter, it became popular to think of services as a good. Consequently, the U.S. goal became raising services up the hierarchy of issues. No one was thinking of telecommunications in particular but of all services in general. The trading of services was, in government terms, a fifth-order problem: it did not matter to many people. In fact, only a few people "in the backwaters" cared about it. The goal became to raise the issue up the policy agenda until it became a second- or third-order problem, thus necessitating that more people pay attention to it.

Geza Feketekuty in the office of the U.S. Trade Representative (USTR) was the "architect" of U.S. government strategy. He took charge of the mission to introduce trade in services onto the agenda of the U.S. government. He ran a masterful strategy successfully, which began by defining services and trade in services, showing that trade in services might be measured and documenting obstacles hampering trade in services. He expanded the circle of people interested in services by sending cablegrams to every U.S. embassy asking what problems they were having with services. Predictably, the embassies responded by asking, "what are services?" Feketekuty sent back lists and then began receiving useful responses, which he then compiled. He got important support in the early 1980s from William Brock, the new USTR under the Reagan Administration. William Brock became convinced of the importance of trade in services and raised the issue everywhere he went. Because Brock and Feketekuty were raising the issue, others were forced to respond.

In the meantime, Feketekuty was continuing the difficult task of persuading the U.S. government to deal with the trade in services issue. The Treasury Department claimed that they owned finance, and therefore services were not their concern. The Department of Commerce declared that services were not important enough for them to deal with but they retained the rights to services anyway. The State Department agreed that because it was an international issue they should probably "own" it. Getting everybody on board was completed.

Concurrently, Feketekuty moved to get the business community on board. With few exceptions, most notably American Express, the business community was not involved. American Express cared about this issue because their business depends on their huge private network. Its day-to-day operations necessitate large information flows regarding credit approvals and fund transfers between offices worldwide.

It was easier to get academics interested. Feketekuty soon recruited a number of well-known academics to begin researching and writing about services. He also started talking to key people in the press, but his efforts were mainly concentrated on government and business.

Efforts to draw attention to the issue of trade in services spread to the international level when the OECD trade committee became involved. Originally member countries claimed that they had no barriers to trade in services. Feketekuty responded by tabling a 500-page list of barriers to U.S. trade in services. This motivated other countries to identify barriers erected by the United States. Collectively, all this activity led quickly to a greater visibility of services. Telecommunications was just one of many services examined. Only later was it perceived to be the key service.

In late 1982, a GATT ministerial meeting was held in Geneva. Previous ministerial meetings had always been used to launch new trade rounds. However, the world was still in recession. It was difficult to hold the system together, much less get a new trade round. The United States started talking about trade and services, but the only result of the Geneva ministerial was an agreement that any country wanting to conduct a self-study of its services industries could do so. They then would be discussed in Geneva. However, Brazil and India, who traditionally opposed the trade in services issue, did not think services should be discussed at the GATT. They argued that services were beyond the jurisdiction of the GATT. It literally took years to determine whether the national studies that countries brought to the GATT were official or unofficial.

To summarize, this period was good because people in business, government, academic, and press communities started to be concerned about trade and services. Some lessons can be learned from this period. First, it is striking how few people were involved in the early stages, proving that it only takes a few to get quite a bit of attention. Second, to get a reaction from busy government officials, one must present them with a document. A document means that someone in government actually has to think about it because they have to respond. Third, because governments and bureaucracies are busy, anyone who writes a good report or speech gets plagiarized. For example, the USTR makes about five speeches a week, too many for each to be completely different. Thus, if one provides good prose, it tends to get used in every speech. Ultimately, the language is accepted as government policy.

Feketekuty was always honest and open, actually detailing his strategy to anyone who would listen. Perhaps, inevitably, everybody thought the United States had a secret plot. The Indian government in particular, invented much more elaborate conspiracy theories than anybody in the United States was even capable of dreaming up. In some sense, the Indians and Brazilians played into the hands of the United States without knowing it; controversy is not always bad. Everybody agrees that when an event is boring, the press does not write about it. When the Indians and Brazilians complained that services were an industrial country ploy, extensive press coverage was ensured. The issue became bigger and bigger. Ultimately, before the Punta del Este ministerial meeting in 1986, the idea was to divide and conquer. Consequently, what started as a large group of developing countries against trade in services and a few industrial countries who were lukewarm ended as strong majority in favor of moving ahead. After reviewing the data in their national studies countries became intrigued by their service sectors. To their great surprise, they found that services played a more significant role in their economies than they had thought. Even the French, who had never been a great friend of services, changed their minds. They began to convince the sub-Saharan/African states that, in fact, the Brazilians and Indians were large service exporters to sub-Saharan Africa and that they were charging them much more than industrial countries. In the end, all but a few of the African states changed their original position.

Finally, 10 countries opposed the concept. Brazil, which always needed money because of the debt crisis, led the opposition, but saw trade in services as a negotiating ploy. The Indians believed trade in services was a bad idea, largely because they were afraid that if their service industries got any more efficient, they would suffer even more unemployment. Therefore, it was as much an employment issue as a trade issue to them.

THE BAD

The second period began with the task of trying to get services, and ultimately telecommunications services, on the negotiating agenda. Brazil, India, and a few other developing countries led the fight. The problem with trade in services was that it was new. No set of codified rules and principles existed, so it was not simply reducing barriers but also determining how to incorporate services into the world economy and global economic rules.

The OECD and others began trying to create a conceptual framework that would ideally cover as many services as possible, modeled so far as possible on the trade principles that already existed within the GATT. Nonetheless, it became fairly clear early that existing GATT articles could not be extended easily to services. In many ways services are similar to goods, but there are important differences. For instance, a tariff on goods is levied at the border. But how do you tariff information flows crossing a border? It is possible but difficult. The situation got more complicated when the United States identified telecommunications as one of the two key services.

Early on, telecommunications and finance were pinpointed as critical. Aviation and tourism were seen as significant too, but it was clear that finance and telecommunications provide the infrastructure for other industries in the coming information age. Many examples exist of the wonderful things that can be traded over telecommunications networks: the cartoon industry in the Philippines, data entry in Korea, American Airlines running its reservation system out of Barbados, and the Polish National Airline running its reservation system out of Atlanta.

The framework agreement being worked out by the OECD began to progress. To everyone's surprise, at the 1988 mid-term review held in Montreal the framework agreement did quite well, although nothing specific was included about telecommunications. An agreement was reached on objectives in terms of what the key issues were, not on what to do. Agriculture and intellectual property, not services, broke down the 1988 talks. In the meantime, telecommunications trade got more attention, so much so that the issue became divisive in the United States.

For this, the United States was to blame. It spent much time and effort without enough consultation with its international partners, particularly the developing countries. In addition, the whole situation related to trade in telecommunications was grossly misunderstood because there was little real telecommunications expertise in the USTR's office, although many people were working on telecommunications. None of the USTR staff were engineers or Ph.D. economists, and not one of them had ever worked in the industry. So, when it came to drafting the telecommunications annex, the USTR had to seek help. The original drafter was a Federal Communications Commission (FCC) lawyer who had assisted during the United States-Canada negotiations. Unfortunately, his draft was so complicated that the U.S. negotiators did not understand the intricacies of their own draft. This made it impossible for them to determine their priorities.

The second mistake was made in attaching the draft to the framework agreement. The framework agreement was developing fairly well at that stage. Negotiators had two choices. They could negotiate separate sectoral agreements for telecommunications, finance, and a few other sectors. This would have allowed a country to sign on just to the framework agreement and not the finance, telecommunications, or aviation sectoral agreements. Presumably like-minded countries, or countries that wanted to go a little farther on the issue of trade in services, would sign, and others would not. The other possibility, the one opted for, was to make telecommunications an annex to the framework agreement. This meant that signatories of the framework agreement were stuck with the annex whether they liked it or not. The two could not be separated. The result was that countries hesitant about telecommunications, finance, etc. (originally there was to be more than one annex) might not sign the framework agreement. Therefore, the language used in the annex got looser and looser, and ultimately the draft became so complicated that it was probably doomed then.

Another problem arose. U.S. business support began to fragment over what they wanted in the agreement. The U.S. Business Council produced a series of drafts for the U.S. government about what the user community or, more particularly, the provider community wanted. The leaders in this effort were General Motors (because of EDS) and IBM. AT&T, originally part of the alliance, switched its position in mid-1990. AT&T then convinced MCI, Sprint and a few others that the U.S. position was untenable; they wanted to pull basic services out of the agreement. This caused consternation at Citibank, EDS, American Express, and even IBM because many of them rely on private networks, which provide basic as well as value-added services. These firms wanted to protect access to their private networks. They feared that the AT&T position would undermine them. The private community was split.

Internal dissension undercut the U.S. negotiators. How far could they go? The more ambitious firms wanted a positive list: the only services that can be excluded from the agreement are those that are positively listed. The AT&T group sought a negative list: only if the service is on the list should it be included. The positive list is more powerful, particularly when new services were emerging. But AT&T worried that it would be impossible to get other countries to agree not to regulate new services because they had not been listed. AT&T's worst-case scenario was that other countries would enter the basic services market in the United States without AT&T being allowed into basic services elsewhere. The FCC would likely have prevented this from happening, but AT&T was concerned, which caused confusion in the U.S. government.

The final major point of contention concerned whether trade in telecommunications services should be handled with universal or conditional most-favored-nation treatment. To get conditional most-favored-nation status, only signatories get the benefits of agreements. The United States urged that only countries that sign should get the benefits of liberalization. Others, particularly the European Community and less developed countries disagreed, saying that signing the agreement should not have anything to do with liberalization: those not wanting to liberalize yet should not have to do so. Liberalization should be extended universally to all GATT members. Confusion reined as the Brussels meeting approached. Furthermore, there were those, such as the Indians and Brazilians, who still wanted to bracket the entire telecommunications annex and eliminate it.

The Brussels ministerial failed mostly over agricultural issues. It was not the United States or Europe that abandoned the talks. The Argentines led mainly the Latin countries out, saying what they had said in Montreal: Without progress on their issues, they would block progress on all issues. Without agriculture, services was hopeless.

THE UGLY

At Brussels, the developing countries continued to oppose the telecommunications annex. Unlike the industrial world, they believed they did not have to talk about trade in telecommunications at the GATT talks. Many developing countries questioned the objectives of the annex and made no promise to comply.

The United States wanted obligations to be as broad as possible and sought a comprehensive agreement. The key debate focused on whether "a party shall not be required to grant market access to service providers, including telecommunications service providers, of other parties other than specified in its schedule." That was the central theme for the United States — market access. India wanted to maintain its freedom to permit selective market access. They did not want to be obligated to allow market access to anyone. Then, how should market access be defined? In this case, it means freedom to provide services, whether they be traded or invested. If one has a service to offer that is competitive, there ought to be a way to provide it.

Definitions, as all negotiators have learned, are crucial to negotiations. If everyone can agree on the definition of an issue as proposed by one country, then that country has won the first battle because logically everything else about the issue follows from there. In addition to the problem with market access, the Canadians, the Japanese, the European Communities, and the United States disagreed on what "offered publicly" should mean. Because of the vaguely defined terms in the annex, what began as an agreement that was about users and the rights of users, became an agreement about what one negotiator saw as the rights of regulators. The focus changed over time.

The United States and the developing countries also disagreed over intracorporate communications. The United States contended that if a corporation happens to have branches or subsidiaries in many countries they should be able to send internal data back and forth. This aspect is important to U.S. businesses. In contrast, the developing countries wanted to reserve the right to determine exactly what corporate communications can or cannot go through their national boundaries.

CONCLUSION

In summary, even if agriculture had not been a problem, the United States made such a jumble of the telecommunications annex it is unclear whether any U.S. negotiators understood their own text and its implications. The breakdown at Brussels may thus prove a blessing in disguise. It will provide time for the United States and other countries to regroup and try again to reach an agreement on services and telecommunications services.

6

Japanese Private Sector and the Uruguay Round: A Case Study of C. Itoh and Company

Shinzo Kobori

This chapter consists of three parts. First, C. Itoh's corporate policies and activities in the information age and what it is doing to cope with changing business circumstances, domestically and globally, will be presented. Second, the Japanese private sector and the Uruguay Round will be discussed. Third, this chapter will address the United States-Japan bilateral trade issue from the Japanese view of the imbalance.

JAPANESE PRIVATE SECTOR AND THE URUGUAY ROUND

During the last week of January 1991, business people from three continents — North America, Europe, and Asia — met in Washington, D.C. Representatives from the business association of Japan, the Keidanden (Economic Business Federation), the German Business Development Institute, the British Center for Business and Industry, and a number of leading U.S. business associations, under the leadership of the National Association of Manufacturers, issued a joint statement that was distributed to the White House, Congress, the prime minister of Japan, and the Japanese Diet and to each of the heads of state. The joint statement essentially stated that they had gathered to stress industrial interests in a successful Uruguay Round.

The Uruguay Round broke down through disagreements over trade in agricultural products, including rice. The Japanese Diet stood firm behind its stand to not permit the importation of rice. In reaction to the result of the Uruguay Round, all agreed that agriculture should not block the efforts that have been spent in the past four years on successful agreements like trade-related intellectual property or trade-related information management. The Japanese business sector is opposed to this Diet resolution because they will lose much if the Uruguay Round fails on the basis of the insistence on agricultural issues. It is hoped that the Japanese government will reconsider the comparative advantage of giving up their unreasonable pledge of absolutely no imports of rice into Japan.

The problem was that important local elections were due to take place during the first week of April 1991. The Liberal Democratic Party (LDP), the government party, was worried about the outcome of these local elections. Although the LDP believed that the Uruguay Round depended on decisions made concerning agricultural issues, including rice, the LDP wanted to postpone their decision regarding agriculture until after the elections. The United States had to have its fast-track negotiating authority extended by Congress. The timing was tight as the request for this extension had to be initiated no later than March 1, 1991. Also, some commitment in general on the part of Japan toward the rice policy had to be indicated to the U.S. Trade Representative and other negotiating parties. The Japanese were working hard so as not to miss this deadline and hoped to be able to persuade the Japanese Diet to reverse this unreasonable resolution.

C. ITOH'S CORPORATE STRATEGY IN THE INFORMATION AGE

C. Itoh is a trading company by nature and has three basic functions: end user, supplier, and operator of information technologies and systems. Many large and small Japanese companies are now end users, having more and more access to technology and information. C. Itoh differs from these other companies in that it not only uses and takes advantage of the advanced and fast information systems, it also conducts commercial transactions in the capacity of a supplier or an operator. These three functions form the basis on which C. Itoh develops its corporate decisions and policies.

C. Itoh as a user of information technologies has four overseas transmission centers serving 150 offices worldwide. One office is the Hughes Fillmore station in Los Angeles, California. The Tokyo office is linked to Los Angeles, from which Tokyo is then linked to New York. All the other offices in the United States, Canada, and Central and Latin America are connected through this link. Links also exist between Tokyo and London, as well as London and New York. London is the link between the Tokyo office and other C. Itoh offices located in Europe, Africa, and the Middle East. Furthermore, transmission centers are located in Hong Kong and Singapore which serve the company's offices in Asia and Oceania. Services provided through this global network include data transmission, telephone service, telex, and facsimile for daily business communication.

Not only is C. Itoh a user of technological advancement, but it is also trying to optimize the use of advanced information technology by becoming a supplier. This means that it must take an aggressive approach to benefit from new business opportunities. With the advent of the information age, infinite, diverse new business opportunities are opening up. C. Itoh is not just a manufacturer of a product, which would certainly restrict the scope of its expansion into entirely unrelated areas, but a user of information technology.

The General Trading Company (GTC), as C. Itoh is also known, does not have any specific, indigenous line of business. Thus, unlike other industries, such as banking (which is strictly supervised by the Ministry of Finance), GTC is not subjected to any direct ministerial control. Nevertheless, because the company conducts business in the telecommunications industry, it comes under some indirect supervision of the Ministry of Post and Telecommunications.

In addition to being an intermediary of trade, C. Itoh has also been working as an organizer. For instance, during the first oil shock, much oil money was accumulated in the Middle East. C. Itoh organized Japanese and international suppliers to supply the desalination plant, which was in jeopardy during the Gulf War. This traditional and well-proven organizational capability and function of GTC is a factor in forming the new information-related consortium. One example is IDC, the new overseas telecommunications business. C. Itoh invited Toyota to become the major shareholder because Toyota wanted to get into information-related activities. The two companies have been working together as exporters of Toyota products in a number of developing countries. As a result, they were already acquainted.

Furthermore, Nippon Telephone and Telegraph has a critical role in helping C. Itoh. C. Itoh has approximately 10 joint ventures with NTT. Yet, C. Itoh is a shareholder in NTT International. In addition, C. Itoh receives technical assistance from NTT. For example, C. Itoh was not technically equipped to operate Japan Communications Satellite Company (JC Sat) effectively, so it sought NTT's help.

The certainty of the positive and defensive approach is coming together when decisions are made concerning the information age. First and foremost, deregulation was an important and timely factor. While waiting for deregulation, efforts focused on studying the work that could be done when telecommunications deregulation became effective. After deregulation was accomplished, JC Sat, a joint venture with Hughes Aircraft in satellite communications, and IDC, a joint venture with Cable and Wireless of the United Kingdom in overseas telecommunications, became the two basic projects of the new common carrier of C. Itoh. C. Itoh took a positive and forward-looking position toward the satellite industry because its relationship with Hughes Aircraft dated to the 1960s, which gave the company strong incentive to go into the satellite business. The project with IDC began later because C. Itoh was uncertain whether deregulation allowed foreign capital investments in IDC. IDC had a difficult time negotiating, not with Cable and Wireless, but with the Japanese gov-ernment. Talks between Prime Ministers Nakasone and Thatcher were very much instrumental in allowing Cable and Wireless to participate in IDC.

All trading companies like to have international cooperation. Therefore, establishing and maintaining international relationships is an important goal of C. Itoh's. Whenever the company goes into new business ventures, it tries to work closely with overseas and international partners. For instance, when entering other networking, data base, or cable access television (CATV) businesses, the company generally looks into joint ventures.

A wide spectrum of new business opportunities in the telecommunications industry exist: new media business, NTT, JC Sat, and videotext and new data bases. C. Itoh has a joint venture with NHK called Media International Corporation (MICO), which was established in June 1990. The main shareholders are, aside from NHK and C. Itoh, the Seibu group, Sumitomo Bank, and DKB Bank. MICO has become controversial because it wants to get into the global software business in competition with other commercial television networks. Television networks were unhappy because the government-owned NHK, as a shareholder of MICO, was becoming a partner with other commercial companies in seeking software business in broadcasting, joint productions of large-scale broadcasting films and videos, and investment in Mongul films. Therefore, despite being in its infancy and being concerned about them, MICO was inviting commercial television companies to become shareholders. However, this may also mean an all-Japan type of operation.

Established in April 1990, the Japan Network Group Corporation is another joint venture with NHK. The Japan Network Group handles radio broadcasting and NHK Japanese programming through CATV in the United States. This service was initiated in New York in June 1990. It is yet to be known how soon that service will be available nationwide.

All in all C. Itoh works closely with such groups as NTT and NHK. Through NHK, C. Itoh establishes joint ventures with local companies. An example of such joint ventures is that of satellite application in Japan's "off schooling" or "cram schools." Cram schools, while not a part of the official school system, are gaining importance because growing numbers of students wanting to go to high school or college would like to have intensive training after hours. Some of the cram schools are well known for their excellent teachers, who are very rare in Japan. Lessons by these teachers are broadcast by satellite all over Japan, so that students all over Japan can have instantaneous access through a television screen, a unique application of satellite software.

Equipment sales and the import and export of videotapes are commercial operations. When IDC decided to install the undersea trans-Pacific submarine cables, C. Itoh's department dealing in nonferrous metal products was awarded a contract to purchase them on behalf of the IDC. Therefore, although the information business is a new business, it also incorporates the traditional concept of trade. As a matter of fact, trade in hardware is also becoming a part of the company's activities.

UNITED STATES-JAPAN TRADE IMBALANCE

The bilateral trade imbalance is now decreasing for the United States. Although the magnitude of the imbalance is still large, definite improvement in the trade gap is seen over the past couple years. In talking about United States-Japan trade imbalance we must mention the issue of Japanese transplants to the United States. Japanese direct investment in the United States started a while ago, but after 1987 the amount increased rapidly and, in turn, exports increased. Initially, Japanese transplants brought with them manufacturing facilities, capital goods, and the components for assembling. Therefore, at first, these transplants were simply to increase Japanese exports, especially in capital goods and components to the United States. However, as time passed, more U.S.-made components were used. This fact is especially true in automobile assembly. The Japanese have begun to increase imports of products made in their U.S. plants to Japan. Nevertheless, this practice touches on the issue of country of origin at the Uruguay Round.

Ricoh's copy machine is one example of this issue. It is designated as a product with the United States as the country of origin, not Japan. This Japanese transplant production in the United States not only works as an export substitution between two countries but also in exporting their transplant products into Europe and other parts of the world. At first, export growth effect took over, but then, substitution of local content increased. Also, in macroeconomic management, Japan is continuing its policy of stimulating economic growth.

The United States, in trying to reduce the trade deficit, has been seeking different macroeconomic approaches, such as continued increase in domestic demand for growth as an economic policy. However, it is unlikely that the United States will approach the Japanese growth rate. The Japanese domestic demand-led economic growth in the foreseeable future until 1995 might be within the range of 3 to 4 percent per year; the U.S. economy will probably not grow that fast.

Such a different approach in macroeconomic management has a big impact on improving the trade imbalance between the two countries.

Another factor is structural reform, as agreed on in the Structural Impediments Initiative. These reforms entail changes that are within the government's reach to solve, whereas other reforms concerning the private sector may not necessarily be what the government can manage. One area of reform that the Japanese government can control or introduce is antitrust enforcement.

In addition, business disclosure is an issue. Recently, the Ministry of Finance made it known that in a publicly held company there should be more disclosure as to what business relations it has with any keiretsu. Under the business disclosure enactment, more information should be disclosed about the business dealings between two companies if they have joint shareholdings or other business joint ventures. Under the joint-shareholding relationship, the business relations, particularly the transaction volume have to be disclosed for scrutiny, and also in order for deregulation to be possible.

Some business practices that do not necessarily come under direct government jurisdiction but are more of a determination on the part of private business are procurement policies and interlocking shareholding. Although there is no sign of permanent adoption of the interlocking shareholding system, it will certainly be subjected to review of its economic efficiency and optimum financial allocation.

Another controversial point of service trade is that of equal opportunity to compete. The Japanese often insist that Japan is an open country and that equal opportunity to compete is available to any company, whether foreign or domestic. Nevertheless, this is not the general perception. In addition to the United States, the European Community (EC), for instance, does not find this equal opportunity competition concept sufficiently convincing The EC would like to insert the "in effect clause," an approach that Japan is opposed to because it would mean a concession on the part of Japan toward the results-oriented managed trade.

In summary, some changes or potential changes can be undertaken by the Japanese economy to improve the trade imbalance with the United States. It is likely that the problem will remain because the bilateral imbalance with the United States is decreasing more slowly than Japan's overall global imbalance. The Japanese trade surplus was increasing so rapidly that at peak it accounted for 4 percent of the gross national product (GNP). However, in 1990 this figure declined to 1 percent of the GNP, which is about $30 billion. In 1992 it again increased to $50 billion and is 4 percent of GNP.

This decrease in trade surplus does not necessarily reflect an improvement or decrease in the bilateral trade imbalance between Japan and the United States. The steady demand in the United States for Japanese capital goods is also a factor. The Economic Planning Agency gathered representatives from business and academia to study this particular point. At the end of December 1990, a report analyzing why the bilateral trade imbalance between Japan and the United States is decreasing so slowly was released. One reason cited is the steady demand in the United States for Japanese capital goods; the structural composition of trade is another reason. Furthermore, the import/export ratio, which peaked in 1987, is still high, or out of balance. The ratio of U.S. exports to Japan to U.S. imports from Japan in 1985 was 1:3. At the same time, the United States was also running a trade deficit with the EC. However, the export ratio of the United States to the EC was 1:1.4 in 1985. It was easier for the United States to manage a trade deficit of 1.4:1 than 3:1. In fact, by 1990, the United States managed to improve the deficit successfully and even recorded a surplus with the EC.

The trade statistics after 1985 show an interesting point. During the period from 1985 to 1990, U.S. imports from Japan and U.S. imports from the EC were almost the same. However, although the United States managed to deal with its deficit with the EC, it failed with its deficit with Japan. Therefore, something has to be done with Japanese imports from the United States. To have a trade ratio of 1:1, Japan will have to import more from the United States. Some projections are that by 1995, the trade ratio can be as low as 1.2 or 1.3 to 1 in favor of Japan, which means a trade gap of approximately $20 billion or less.

In conclusion, trade figures show slow but steady progress in the improvement of the United States-Japan trade situation. Trade in exports from Japan to the United States of telecommunications equipment in 1985 was worth ¥306 billion and ¥308 billion in 1989. Hence, exports remained about the same. Nevertheless, the U.S. exports to Japan in telecommunications equipment went from ¥30 billion in 1986 to ¥56 billion in 1989. In 1985, Japanese imports from the United States valued ¥30 billion, which went up to ¥56 billion in 1989. Although the figure itself is far from satisfactory, imports from the United States did account for the largest share of Japanese imports. Of the total imports of telecommunications equipment into Japan in 1989, the U.S. exports of ¥56 billion to Japan accounted for 64 percent — by far the largest share. This trend, if it continues, should amend the imbalance situation.

CONCLUSION

The example of C. Itoh presents a case of the role of a Japanese private company in the information age. C. Itoh recognizes the enormous amount of promises telecommunications development can bring to the future of Japan.

With respect to the United States-Japan bilateral trade gap, many factors are involved, and a solution will require much work and commitment from both countries. Nevertheless, the trend seems to show positive progress. If both sides continue to work together, there is hope for improved trade relations between the United States and Japan, who are both striving to keep abreast of the rapidly changing technological world.

7

Trade in Information Services in Asia, ASEAN, and the Pacific: Conceptual Issues and Policy Examples

Marcellus S. Snow

This chapter will detail the most vital sector of international trade in services, namely telecommunications and information services. Services trade as a whole has increased greatly in recent years and has challenged the models, assumptions, and conclusions derived from earlier international trade theories, which were more suitable for trade in goods than trade in services.

I will first view telecommunications services not in isolation but rather as part of the rich matrix of information-based services that have revolutionized international trade and ushered in the information age. The intellectual development of the role of information in the economy and in the process of economic development will be traced briefly.

Next, the major trade issues as they relate to information-based services are discussed. Experts disagree and are uncertain about the definition and role of trade in services in national income accounting and in economic growth and development. These uncertainties are particularly acute for information-based services. The most important such issue deals with the tendency to treat some types of international trade as direct foreign investment (DFI). The role of various international organizations — particularly the General Agreement on Tariffs and Trade (GATT) and the International Telecommunication Union (ITU) — in fostering and regulating international trade in services will be examined as they relate to the development of ideas, policy, and regulation of trade in information services. Other issues mentioned include transborder data flow (TBDF), standard setting, and the merger of telecommunications and computing technologies.

Finally, this chapter presents a case study of the member states of the Association of Southeast Asian Nations (ASEAN), which recently cooperated with scholars from the United States and elsewhere by examining improved trade and economic relations between its six member states — Brunei, Indonesia, Malaysia, the Philippines, Singapore, and Thailand — and the United States.

CONCEPTUAL UNDERPINNINGS OF TELECOMMUNICATIONS AND INFORMATION SERVICES

The notion of information as an economic commodity developed gradually following the Industrial Revolution. Information is more easily characterized by reference to the sectors of the economy in which it predominates than by an explicit definition. It is only in a technical setting — electrical engineering and computer sciences, in particular — that seminal work by noneconomists such as Shannon and Weaver (1949) gave rise to formal definitions of information content, such as the bit.

By the mid-1970s, economists such as Machlup and Arrow were instrumental in gaining the reluctant acceptance by the economics profession that information was a formal subdiscipline. An important milestone was Porat's (1977) multivolume study of the role of information in the U.S. economy, which followed work by Machlup and used national income accounting data in input-output techniques. Porat's study, commissioned by the U.S. Department of Commerce, concluded that the share of U.S. gross national product attributable to the information sector amounted to 21 percent in 1967, the latest year for which he was able to assemble sufficiently precise data. All subsequent research indicates that this figure has increased significantly since that time, in the United States and elsewhere. Methodological treatments drawing on Porat's work have been carried out for a number of countries and regions, including several in Asia and the Pacific (see Jussawalla, Lamberton, & Karunarantne 1988).

The information sector has served as a barometer of structural change in the process of economic development. In fact, many economists and other authorities argue that the rise of an information sector in the industrialized countries of the late twentieth century — one which by now exceeds the output of the manufacturing sector in all such countries — constitutes an information or communications revolution comparable in scope and import with the Industrial Revolution of the nineteenth century. It is the Industrial Revolution that, aided by steam power, the factory system, and various other technical and managerial innovations, first raised the contribution of the manufacturing sector to the economic output of the wealthier nations above that of agriculture.

Thus it is almost a tautology to note that developing countries lag behind their industrialized neighbors by the extent to which their economies fail to use, produce, import, and export information-intensive goods and services. Economic policymakers, practitioners, and theoreticians agree today that any successful strategy of economic development must be based in large part on the information sector. Until the early 1980s, however, this unanimity did not prevail: rather, it was the view of a small but growing and vocal minority. The patient, astute, and expert advocacy of this information lobby eventually prevailed. Previously, national and international lending institutions, such as the U.S. Agency for International Development (USAID) and the World Bank, had exhibited considerable skepticism toward the role of information infrastructure in the process of economic development. This skepticism had its roots in the invisibility and incorporality of information and telecommunications services vis-à-vis the visual splendor of more tangible sectors, such as agriculture, education, energy, health, and transportation.

Today's consensus, as noted above, indicates the necessity of information and telecommunications in the more complete establishment of a market economy to replace barter and the subsistence agriculture in the rural areas of the developing world. Information infrastructure is increasing recognition as a vital prerequisite for economic development rather than merely a desirable side effect (Snow 1985). Telecommunications links and services in particular act as the nerve center of the modern industrial economy, and the information sector can be analogized as the brain in which that center is located.

Information is difficult to define, and its manifold properties lie to a considerable extent in the eye of the beholder. For this reason, information is more trenchantly characterized by reference to the industries in which it appears to predominate. According to the U.S. Department of Commerce, numerous industries are of importance in services exported by the United States. These are accounting, advertising, banking, communications (including telecommunications), computers, construction, education, engineering, employment, franchising, health, insurance, law, motion pictures, shipping (including air transport), and tourism (Krause 1982, p. 57). Casual reflection suggests that a salient aspect of each of these industries, with the exception of construction, is their intensive use of information as a factor of production. Indeed, "international transactions in services tend to be organized around information and its exploitation" (Hindley & Smith 1984; quoted in Lee, [Tsao] 1988, p. 120).

TRADE ISSUES IN INFORMATION-BASED SERVICES

Following are some important issues that have arisen among countries importing and exporting services with a considerable information content. As was pointed out previously, telecommunications must be considered within the broader setting of information, and few, if any, internationally traded services are not substantially based on "information and its exploitation."

Trade in Services versus Direct Foreign Investment

Until recently the issue of defining international trade in information-intensive services has been skirted by various stratagems. International telecommunications circuits linking two countries, for example, were idealized as consisting of two parts. One half-circuit proceeded from country A to the hypothetical midpoint of the link (in mid-ocean for a cable or in mid-orbit for a geosynchronous communications satellite) and then back to country A. A second half-circuit was defined analogously for country B. Thus, no trade took place because, at least conceptually, no service "flowed" from one country to the other. The exchange of services, such as it was, was idealized as taking place either in mid-ocean or 36,000 km above the equator.

More recent efforts to define international trade in services and to relate it to the confusingly similar phenomenon of DFI have come closer to realization. The Organization for Economic Cooperation and Development (OECD), for example, defines traded services as "services essentially produced in one country and paid for by residents of another country" (Aronson & Cowhey 1988, p. 239). Stern and Hoekman (1988), in particular, point out the many conceptual issues still needing to be solved relating to the nature of trade and investment in information-based services. Lee and Naya (1988) advance useful arguments for DFI as a supplement to, or substitute for, trade in services in the process of economic development.

First, they differentiate between services trade and DFI by distinguishing three ways in which international service transactions can occur: resident firms or individuals provide services to nonresident firms or individuals across national boundaries; resident firms or individuals provide services to nonresident firms or individuals within national boundaries; and some services, that is, the use of intangible properties, are transmitted across national boundaries through contractual arrangements (Lee & Naya 1988, p. 29). These types of transactions do not constitute DFI in services since they "do not require the establishment of foreign affiliates" or "the long-term movement of factors of production" (Lee & Naya, 1988).

DFI contrasts in important ways with trade in services. It is the inseparability of production and consumption in trade in services that "accounts for the importance of DFI as a means of selling services in foreign markets" (p. 30). Recent increases in DFI in services, as well as rises in trade in services, can be traced to conventional movements of relative factor endowments as well as changes in technology and transportation costs.

It is the function of the foreign affiliate in minimizing the transaction cost of direct trade that is the major factor in determining the mix of DFI and trade in services that is observed:

> Establishing a service affiliate in a foreign country, which is the purpose of DFI, is a way of reducing the transaction cost of exporting service. They can be provided by the affiliate to firms and individuals residing in the foreign country, and the international movement of providers or receivers of services need not take place for every transaction. The initial transaction cost of establishing the affiliate can be amortized over its life, and consequently services can be provided at a lower cost than if they were exported by the parent firm (p. 31).

If economies of scale are exhausted sooner for a service firm in the exporting country than for its various service establishments in host countries, the DFI in services may be preferred to trade. In this sense a foreign affiliate is "simply an establishment located in a foreign country" (p. 31). DFI is a sensitive issue for developing countries. They regard the concept of national treatment, namely, nondiscrimination between foreign and domestic service suppliers, as applicable to goods rather than services. In addition, infant-industry arguments are advanced by developing countries to oppose the establishment of foreign-owned service affiliates. These views contrast starkly with those of the United States, the European Community (EC), and Japan, all of which favor nondiscriminatory DFI services as well as goods (Koekkoek 1988, p. 154).

In according separate treatment to trade in services and DFI in services one can, finally, distinguish between

> The competitiveness of a country in service industries and the competitiveness of its firms in the same industries in the world market. A country's comparative advantage in service industries is location-specific, whereas firms' competitiveness in the world market is firm-specific and not bound to a particular location (Lee & Naya 1988, p. 31).

Other researchers (for example, Aronson & Cowhey 1988, p. 238) argued that this and other definitional issues would be used at the present Uruguay Round of the GATT by opponents of trade liberalization. They would, it was predicted, insist on complete definitional coverage of trade and DFI in services before agreeing to any substantive trade agreements. The United States, by contrast, maintained that the insights of the GATT discussions themselves would iterate into progressive clarity on definitional issues as the talks proceed. Although they noted a "general consensus that services are becoming more tradable," Aronson and Cowhey conceded that "there can be no GATT agreement on services without de facto treatment of investment" (pp. 239–40; emphasis omitted).

Transborder Data Flow

Transborder data flow (TBDF) became a subject of vital concern and fre-quent conferences and consultations among academics, policy-makers, and the international user community long before it was well understood or explained in the context of international trade theory. Some of the best analyses to date are those of Cheah (1984), Jussawalla (1984), and Jussawalla and Cheah (1986).

Typical examples of TBDF include data transmitted for commercial purposes by using public international data channels, the transmission over private leased lines of data from a developing to a developed country for storage or processing in the developed country, and data communications between the headquarters of a multinational corporation and one of its overseas subsidiaries.

Ostensibly, concern with TBDF has often been couched in terms of privacy protection, cultural autonomy, or national sovereignty by countries inclined to restrict such flows by various regulations. Dispassionate analysis generally suggests a hidden agenda, namely, protectionist economic motives akin to more conventional barriers in international trade of goods.

It has been suggested that concern with TBDF is in many instances misplaced. Preoccupation with "content rather than conduit" masks the underlying issue, which is guaranteed market access to data bases and transmission facilities across international boundaries:

> Most corporate data flows with relative ease between countries and most problems are resolved amicably when they arise. If market access is assured, most information flow problems will take care of themselves. Putting too much emphasis on the free flow of data could overload the [GATT] talks and cause a backlash against market access (Aronson & Cowhey 1988, pp. 250–51).

As interconnection and access increase globally, the increased temptation to tax, regulate, or otherwise impede the free flow of information will tend to isolate the countries doing so, particularly as broadband integrated services digital networks (ISDNs) proliferate internationally (p. 251).

Trade in Services and International Organizations

The GATT and the ITU, in particular, find themselves in a jurisdictional battle that may not be resolved in the near future. The issue sharpened somewhat during the World Administrative Tele-graph and Telephone Conference (WATTC) held in Melbourne in late 1988 under ITU auspices, at the same time that GATT negotia-tors in Uruguay were grappling with the trade in services issue.

An ITU official assured a telecommunications gathering the following month that the WATTC had "achieved a working com-promise in a cooperative spirit," and that no winners had emerged. He saw the ITU's hand in the important trade in services area as having been strengthened with respect to the GATT machin-ery (Snow 1989b). Other observers were less sanguine about the outcome.

An industry representative characterized the ITU/GATT dichoto-my succinctly:

> It is clear that neither the ITU nor the GATT could effectively usurp the duties of the other.... However ... this juris-dictional issue is symbolic of the greater issue we all face in our own countries: to what extent should telecommunications be closely regulated or left to develop under more general market forces? This is a question each sovereign nation must face, and the aggregate will undoubtedly be reflected in the balance of power struck between the ITU and the GATT (Theus, 1989, pp. 114–15; emphasis omitted).

Jurisdictional disputes among international organizations are nothing new, and to a certain extent the tension and counterpoint of their shifting priorities and responsibilities can be salutary to them all. In addition, entities other than the ITU and the GATT also have interests and competence that impinge on trade in services. The OECD, for example, has recently concerned itself with TBDF and the associated issues of privacy and national sovereignty. Snow and Jussawalla (1989), under OECD auspices, undertook an explicit examination of trade, technology, and interdependence.

Another emerging forum for the consideration of trade in services questions is the EC, which is presently preparing for the harmoni-zation of its 12 members into a stronger federal union at the end of 1992. Originally, the EC and its commission had little interest or jurisdiction in telecommunications trade matters. In the early 1980s, however, the European Commission became concerned that the fragmentation of European telecommunications put the EC at a disadvantage with respect to the United States and Japan. Several initiatives resulted from this realization:

a protracted antitrust suit against IBM;
legal action against member states for discrimination against
  each other in telecommunications equipment procurement;

the formation of the European Strategic Program in Information Technology (Esprit), a ten-year (1984–93) collaborative
research program designed to help European information
technology become "competitive on world markets within a
decade";

the formation of the program for research and development
in Advanced Communications Technologies in Europe
(RACE) in 1985 to foster the research and development
needed for the EC-wide introduction of ISDN by 1995;

the establishment in 1985 of the European Research Coordinating Agency (Eureka), which is "designed to strengthen
European productivity and competitiveness through
cooperation of firms and research institutions in the area of
high technology," including telecommunications; and

the issuance in 1987 by the EC Commission of the Green Paper
on the Development of the Common Market for Telecommunications Services and Equipment, arguing for harmonization and liberalization in Western European telecommunications services and equipment (Aronson &
Cowhey 1988, pp. 49, 201–3; Noam 1989, pp. 292–93;
Commission of the European Communities 1987).

Merger of Computing and Telecommunications

Governments have historically structured and regulated
telecommunications and computing in quite different ways. Prior to
the mid-1970s virtually all forms of commercial public telecommunications were owned, operated, and regulated by the state, generally
through a Post, Telephone, and Telegraph ministry. Computing, by
contrast, arose and continues to thrive in an environment of laissez-
faire in virtually all nonsocialist industrialized countries. Nora and
Minc (1980), writing for the French government, were among the
first researchers to point out that telecommunications and computing, despite their vastly different regulatory regimes, were
steadily merging from the standpoint of their technologies.

The way in which the regulatory apparatus in each country
accommodates this merger will have obvious consequences for
international trade in services. If the stricter regulatory regime for
telecommunications were to predominate in the merging arena of
telecommunications and computing technology, less international
trade in services would result, all other factors being equal. Conversely, if the vastly more liberal regime governing computing
services were applied, international trade in services would be
encouraged.

In general, the reaction to this asymmetric pattern of regulation
across merging technologies appears to have been to liberalize the

regulation of telecommunications rather than to tighten the regulation of computing. Thus, international trade in both telecommunications goods and services has benefited.

In the United States, this pattern has been borne out most clearly in the Computer I, Computer II and Computer III proceedings conducted by the Federal Communications Commission (FCC). In its Computer I decision in 1967, the FCC prohibited the direct entry of the American Telephone & Telegraph Company (AT&T) into data processing, but it permitted other common carriers to access that market under a number of regulatory safeguards, such as the establishment of arm's-length subsidiaries. At issue in Computer II was the distinction between basic and enhanced services, which involved the development of new computing technology allowing the decentralization of computing functions to "intelligent" telecommunications terminals. Enhanced services were left unregulated, and the old data processing/communications dichotomy was abandoned. The Computer III inquiry, begun in 1985, unfolded in the context of the divestiture of the Bell system into seven regional operating companies. AT&T received some measure of pricing flexibility in new services and had some of its separate subsidiary restrictions removed.

This regulatory cognizance of the merger of telecommunications and computing has resulted in liberalized regimes in other countries as well (see Snow 1986; Bruce, Cunard, & Director 1986). Most dramatically, both Japan and the United Kingdom privatized their major domestic telecommunications carriers in 1985 and subjected them to some degree of domestic competition. In addition, the Green Paper of the European Communities states: "the long-term convergence of telecommunications with audio-visual technologies must be taken into account, in addition to the current convergence between the telecommunications and data-processing sectors" (Commission of the European Communities 1987, p. 14). Further, it notes the "blurring of the traditional boundary lines between [basic and value-added] services" (p. 33) and makes appropriate regulatory suggestions.

Likewise, West Germany's Witte Report acknowledges the regulatory consequences of disappearing distinctions between various service categories: "the principle of competition is in future to be the rule in telecommunications while the public provider monopoly will be the exception that has to be duly justified (Germany 1988, p. 4).

Standard Setting and the Integrated
Services Digital Networks

The ambitious plans for global ISDN services by the mid-1990s or earlier illustrate the extent to which standard setting at the national and international levels can influence the extent and composition of information-based services in international trade. Economically and technically optimal standard setting must follow a perilous course between two undesirable extremes. If too many standards are imposed too soon, creativity and market forces may be stifled; if too few standards are imposed too late, economically wasteful duplication, disorder, and fragmentation may result (Snow 1989b, p. 171).

Seen differently, the market, technical, and regulatory forces are such that even when everyone can benefit from standardization, there is no assurance that the optimal standard, or indeed any standard, will be chosen. Standards may be used strategically by firms and regulatory bodies for competitive purposes. These entities may promote either relative incompatibility or compatibility, depending on whether they wish to impede the spread of rival technologies and systems or to promote their own. Patterns of standardization in the United States and Western Europe are instructive in this regard. In the United States, the standardization previously inherent in the AT&T system has been gradually replaced by a regime under which substantial autonomy is enjoyed by all participants. Voluntary standard setting has become more prominent in this process. In Western Europe, however, where each country previously enjoyed considerable leeway in the establishment of its own standards, countries are now relinquishing a good deal of that independence in order to benefit from more rapid technical change (Besen & Saloner 1989, pp. 219–20).

A common U.S. reaction to early European proposals for ISDN design standards, for example, was that those standards were too restrictive. Although such early hesitations may appear in retrospect to have been overstated, they do bear an important kernel of truth. The concern persists that the design of the ISDN through restrictions on user access, for example, can be used to "limit the competition faced by the operators of a transmission network," thereby giving rise to conflicts between users and suppliers. Whereas users typically want to maximize their service options, providers often wish to limit such options in order to maximize their operating efficiencies and minimize their financial losses to competitors (Besen & Saloner 1989, pp. 213–14).

U.S. concerns respecting overly strict standard setting for the ISDN presently center less on the threat of hegemonic systems (Noam 1986) than on the very real possibility of a kind of benign mercantilism that would affect U.S. interests adversely in three primary ways. First, European information companies having agreed among themselves, could influence the establishment of standards and software, making it easier for European equipment manufacturers to compete against IBM. Large European users would have local or European alternatives to IBM's information systems. Second, data communications, constrained by the pace of ISDN installation, would develop more slowly. Since Europe lags in this market, it would have a respite to catch up. Third, national producers in Europe can be favored by an ISDN that influences the mix of equipment sales and other procurement patterns (Aronson & Cowhey 1988, pp. 187–91).

Policy of the GATT Uruguay Round toward Trade in Services

Despite its lack of a comprehensive agreement to date, the Uruguay Round of the GATT has made considerable progress. (For details, see Center for the Study of International Economic Relations 1989; GATT 1989). Two major trends are the large number of developing countries that have undertaken the unilateral liberalization of trade restrictions and changes in approach to the GATT, in particular the increased participation of developing countries in the Uruguay Round. For example, 170 of the first 400 proposals were put forward by developing countries. Measures undertaken by South Korea, for example, include a commitment to reduce tariffs at an annual rate of 8 percent through 1993 and a three-year plan to free all manufactured goods and many agricultural products from discretionary import licensing.

Early in the Uruguay Round, GATT representatives formed 15 negotiating groups, one of which was assigned the topic of trade in services. It adopted the following 10 subject areas for discussion and negotiation: definition and statistical issues, principles and rules, multilateral arrangements, existing arrangements relating to services, measures and practices affecting the expansion of trade in services, foreign investment, international labor mobility, national treatment, receiver mobility, and the right of establishment in host countries of foreign affiliates of multinational firms providing internationally traded services.

The GATT's trade in services group met for one week during the summer of 1989. Most of its deliberations focused on the telecommunications and construction sectors. Regarding telecommunications, the majority felt that GATT policies relating to trade in services should initially apply only to enhanced services and not to basic services. The close connection between telecommunications goods and services was noted and examined as the intimate link between the telecommunications sector and other service industries such as banking and tourism. Representatives of some countries stressed the security and privacy aspects of telecommunications flows, while several representatives from developing countries emphasized the need for subsidizing rural telephone services by excess revenues from more remunerative activities.

In December 1990 at Brussels, the chair of the ministerial meeting at GATT's Trade Negotiations Committee stated that disagreements among negotiating partners were sufficiently strong to prevent the conclusion of the Uruguay Round at that meeting, reportedly "due to EC inflexibility in meeting the demand of the U.S. and Cairns Group [of 14 agricultural exporting countries] for an internationally agreed program of reform than would ensure far-reaching reductions to farm subsidies," estimated at $220 billion a year worldwide (Dullforce 1991, p. 1). Informal negotiations and contacts continued through early February 1991, when the GATT's director-general announced that a consensus in favor of successfully concluding the Uruguay Round remained among governments (p. 1). Much depended on whether President George Bush would ask the U.S. Congress, by its March 1 deadline, for a extension of his fast-track authority to negotiate trade agreements.

TRADE IN INFORMATION SERVICES:
ASEAN COUNTRIES AS A CASE STUDY

A recent comprehensive report (Naya et al. 1989) on economic relations between the United States and the six ASEAN countries devotes considerable attention to issues of trade in services and direct foreign investment. Snow (1989a), in an article amplifying his role in the project, discusses banking telecommunications, and intellectual property as objects of trade in services between the United States and ASEAN. The report is important because, although it is technically unofficial, it was financed by the USAID on the U.S. side and by the United Nations Development Program on the ASEAN side. Technically termed the ASEAN-United States Initiative, the project's final report was written by scholars at the East-West Center and University of Hawaii in Honolulu and at the Institute for Southeast Asian Studies in Singapore.

The report's chapter on trade in services begins by noting that U.S. service industries in recent years have contributed to a rapid rise in DFI, increasing the services share of total U.S. DFI from 20 percent to 25 percent in the eight years preceding 1983. As to the definition of traded services, the report views them as "transborder transactions by service industries which do not require the establishment of foreign affiliates through DFI" (Naya et al. 1989, p. 66). Following this definition, the ASEAN-U.S. researchers determine that DFI in services and sales of foreign affiliates are "far more important than trade in services for the United States" (p. 67). The issue is

More the question of whether US firms in the service industries have a firm-specific competitive edge not bound to a particular location and less whether the United States has a comparative advantage in service industries. . . . [A] country's comparative advantage and the competitiveness of its firms are not the same because firms in certain industries which are highly mobile internationally may be very competitive in foreign countries even though their native country, given its immobile factor endowments, does not have a comparative advantage in these industries. Thus, it is quite possible that, although there has not been any significant change in the comparative advantage of the United States with respect to service industries, some of the firms in these industries have recently gained a competitive edge which allows them to compete in the global market for services (p. 68).

Given a definition of trade in services as narrow as that proposed by the ASEAN-United States Initiative, DFI in services should be considered as intimately related to trade issues in conceptual and policy settings.

The report highlights the most important sectoral contributions to trade in services in each ASEAN country. In Brunei, the dominant sector is government services, including wholesale and retail trade. In Indonesia, shipping is the dominant sector, most of which is related to the petroleum industry. Malaysia's primary traded services sector is travel, while "other services," including construction, operating expenses, commissions, and fees, are the dominant traded service category in the Philippines. Tourism furnishes the highest earnings for Singapore's trade with the United States; Singapore also attracts by far the largest amount of U.S. DFI in services among the ASEAN countries. U.S. DFI in services amounted to $529 million in 1985, or 27.9 percent of total U.S. investment in Singapore. Thailand exhibits deficits in services trade with all its major trading partners except for other ASEAN nations; the only surpluses are in the areas of travel and tourism (Naya et al. 1989, pp. 68–69).

As to government policies toward services trade, the variation among ASEAN countries is considerable. The ASEAN-U.S. researchers classified these policies with respect to the following criteria:

national treatment — nondiscriminatory applicability of domestic laws and regulations to domestic and foreign firms;

least restrictive regulations — regulation in the least restrictive manner possible in cases where regulation is indeed justified;

nondiscrimination — the application of the most-favored nation criterion to services;

right to sell — allowing market access to foreign service firms;

transparency — open and unambiguous regulations and laws
restricting trade; and

subsidies — identifying their distortive effects and adverse
influence on producers of services (p. 70).

Judging by these criteria, the ASEAN-U.S. researchers found
unjustified barriers to trade in the following sectors of the ASEAN
countries indicated:

Brunei — no barriers;

Indonesia — insurance, leasing, motion pictures, franchising, and maritime transportation;

Malaysia — advertising, insurance, leasing, and motion pictures;

Philippines — banking, franchising, insurance, motion
pictures, air and maritime transportation, and advertising;

Singapore — insurance, maritime transportation, and
banking; and

Thailand — advertising, banking, insurance, leasing, motion
pictures, and air transportation (pp. 70–72).

On the basis of these criteria and nationally imposed barriers, the
ASEAN-United States Initiative report makes the following policy
recommendations for both the ASEAN countries and the United
States, as applicable: greater liberalization and an enhanced role for
private enterprise in the information sector; revision of U.S. antitrust
laws to facilitate trade in services by U.S. firms; relaxation of foreign
equity control on foreign investment in ASEAN countries; relaxation
of controls on foreign banking; continued emphasis on U.S. export
consciousness; relaxation of limits on professional services by
foreigners; reduction of marketing restrictions in the ASEAN
countries; and development of better theory and data (Naya et al.
1989, pp. 76–78; Snow 1989a, pp. 39–41).

The ASEAN-U.S. researchers predicted that the following
major benefits would flow from implementing these recommendations:

a transition in the ASEAN countries to export-oriented, high-
growth trade patterns stressing comparative advantage,
production efficiency, and technology transfer rather than
self-sufficiency and import substitution;

greater allocative efficiency in the United States and ASEAN,
and absolutely and relatively lower producer service prices;

a vital role for the liberalized information sector in stimulating
overall economic growth, particularly through telecommunications in establishing broader and more efficient
markets;

greater government efficiency due to market incentives and
potential competition from the private sector in services
traditionally offered by governments;

greater technology transfer, aided by trade in high-technology
services; and

desirable sociocultural effects, such as the development of a
stronger middle class, reduction of bribery and corruption,
and the replacement of authoritarian and centralized political cultures by pluralistic democracies (Naya et al. 1989,
pp. 78–80; Snow 1989a, pp. 42–44).

Somewhat reflecting the recommendations of Aronson and
Cowhey (1988) with respect to the GATT framework as a whole, the
ASEAN-U.S. researchers propose an umbrella agreement between
ASEAN and the United States that would provide for more specific
bilateral agreements, all of which would be consistent with GATT.
Indeed, bilateral ASEAN-U.S. trade and investment agreements
could complement the GATT talks and "provide an exemplary
framework in certain areas." Individual accords could include, most
comprehensively, an ASEAN-U.S. free-trade agreement. Other topics
might include subsidies; double taxation; intellectual property rights;
investment; services; tariffs; nontariff barriers; and safeguards
codifying standards and establishing disciplinary measures. The
services agreement would deal on a priority basis with definition of
services; nondiscriminatory treatment; transparency; dispute settlement; and enforcement (Naya et al. 1989, pp. 190–96).

CONCLUSIONS

The foregoing considerations suggest a number of policy conclusions regarding international trade in telecommunications and
information services.

Telecommunications services must be seen in the larger context
of the information services sector, indeed as the nerve center of that
sector. The growth of the information sector is in turn fueling the
qualitative transformation of the late twentieth century world
economy. Nearly all internationally traded services are information
based.

DFI and trade in services are intimately linked and should be
considered in concert for purposes of definition, model construction,
data gathering, and policy analysis. Services are becoming increasingly tradable without the intermediation of foreign service establishments. A multinational firm may be competitive in the world
market for certain services even though the country in which it has
its headquarters does not enjoy a comparative advantage in trading
those same services.

Because it concentrates on content rather than conduit, TBDF as an issue often masks other, more basic concerns, such as protectionism. Assured market access will help most information flow problems sort themselves out.

The GATT is the primary forum for facilitating freer international trade services, although the ITU, the OECD, the United Nations, and the EC have also been helpful. The present Uruguay Round is progressing gradually but perceptibly toward formally incorporating trade in services into GATT's negotiating and treaty machinery.

The inexorable merger of telecommunications and computing technologies and services has led to deregulation and liberalization of telecommunications in virtually all industrialized countries. This trend is gradually liberalizing trade in all information-based services.

Standard setting for information services such as ISDN that are too strict can impede international trade in service. Standard setting can be used by governments to prevent foreign competition or to favor preferred domestic suppliers.

As a recent in-depth study of ASEAN-U.S. economic relations articulates, liberalized trade in services is a vital factor in sustaining economic growth, efficiency, and development in industrialized and industrializing countries alike.

REFERENCES

Aronson, Jonathan D. and Peter F. Cowhey. 1988. *When Countries Talk: International Trade in Telecommunications Services.* Cambridge, MA: Ballinger.

Besen, Stanley M. and Garth Saloner. 1989. "The Economics of Telecommunications Standards." In *Changing the Rules: Technological Change, International Competition, and Regulation in Economics,* edited by Robert W. Crandall and Kenneth Flamm, pp 177–220. Washington, DC: Brookings Institution.

Bruce, Robert R., Jeffrey P. Cunard, and Mark D. Director. 1986. *From Telecommunications to Electronic Services: A Global Spectrum of Definitions, Boundary Lines and Structures.* Boston, MA: Butterworths.

Center for the Study of International Economic Relations, the University of Western Ontario. 1989. "The Uruguay Round and Beyond: The Final Report." London, Ontario, Canada, July 20, press release.

Cheah, Chee-wah. 1984. "An Econometric Analysis of TDF Regulation," *Transnational Data Report* 8, (8) (December 8), pp. 475–79.

Commission of the European Communities. 1987. "Towards a Dynamic European Economy: Green Paper on the Development of the Common Market for Telecommunications Services and Equipment," COM(87) 290 final, Brussels. Mimeographed.

Dullforce, William. 1991. "Hopes Rising for GATT Salvage Job," *Financial Times,* February 1, p. 1.

GATT. 1989. "News of the Uruguay Round of Multilateral Trade Negotiations," July 7, pp. 6–8. Geneva: GATT, Information and Media Relations Division.

Germany (Federal Republic). 1988. *Federal Ministry of Posts and Telecommunications. Reform of the Postal and Telecommunications System in the Federal Republic of Germany.* Heidelberg: R. V Decker's Verlag, G. Schenck.

Hindley, Brian and Alasdair Smith. 1984. "Comparative Advantage and Trade in Services." *The World Economy* 7, (4) (December), pp. 369–89.

Jussawalla, Meheroo. 1984. "International Trade and Welfare Implications of Transborder Data Flow." In *Policy Research in Telecommunications: Proceedings from the Eleventh Annual Telecommunications Policy Research Conference,* edited by Vincent Mosco, pp. 400–10. Norwood, NJ: Ablex.

Jussawalla, Meheroo and Che-wah Cheah. 1986. *The Calculus of International Communications: A Study of the Political Economy of Transborder Data Flows.* Boulder, CO: Libraries Unlimited.

Jussawalla, Meheroo, Donald M. Lamberton, and Neil D. Karunaratne, eds. 1988. *The Cost of Thinking: Information Economies of Ten Pacific Countries.* Norwood, NJ: Ablex.

Koekkoek, K. A. 1988. "Trade in Services, the Developing Countries, and the Uruguay Round." *World Economy* 11, (1) (March), pp. 151–55.

Krause, Lawrence B. 1982. *U.S. Economic Policy toward the Association of Southeast Asian Nations: Meeting the Japanese Challenge.* Washington, DC: Brookings Institution.

Lee, Chung H. and Seiji Naya. 1988. "Patterns of Trade and Investment in Services in the Asia-Pacific Region." In *Trade and Investment in Services in the Asia-Pacific Region,* edited by Chung H. Lee and Seiji Naya, pp. 27–52. Boulder, CO: Westview Press.

Lee, (Tsao) Yuan. 1988. "ASEAN-U.S. Trade in Services: An ASEAN Perspective." In *ASEAN-U.S. Economic Relations: Changes in the Economic Environment and Opportunities,* edited by Tan Loong Hoe and Narongchai Akrasanee, pp. 115–45. Singapore: Institute for Southeast Asian Studies.

Naya, Seiji, Chung Lee, and William James. 1989. *ASEAN-U.S. Initiative: Assessment and Recommendations for Improved Economic Relations.* Honolulu: East-West Center; Singapore: Institute for Southeast Asian Studies.

Noam, Eli M. 1989. "International Telecommunications in Transition." In *Changing the Rules: Technological Change, International Competition, and Regulation in Communications,* edited by Robert W. Crandall and Kenneth Flamm, pp. 257–97. Washington, DC: Brookings Institution.

____. 1986. "The Political Economy of ISDN: European Network Integration vs American System Configuration." Paper prepared for Sixth International Conference on Forecasting and Analysis for Business Planning in the Information Age, December, Tokyo.

Nora, Simon and Alain Minc. 1980. *The Computerization of Society.* Cambridge, MA: MIT Press.

Porat, Marc U. 1977. *The Information Economy,* 9 vols. Washington, DC: U.S. Department of Commerce, Office of Telecommunications.

Shannon, Claude E. and Warren Weaver. 1949. *The Mathematical Theory of Communication.* Urbana, IL: University of Illinois Press.

Snow, Marcellus S. 1989a. "Facilitating ASEAN-U.S. Trade and Direct Foreign Investment in Information Services: Alternative Policies and Their Effects," *ASEAN Economic Bulletin,* 6, (1) (July), pp. 31–45.

____. 1989b. "Pacific Telecommunications Connectivity," *Telecommunications Policy,* 13 (2) (June), pp. 170–71.

____, ed. 1986. *Marketplace for Telecommunications: Regulation and Deregulation in Industrialized Democracies.* New York: Longman.

___. 1985. "Regulation to Deregulation: The Telecommunications Sector and Industrialization, With Evidence from the Pacific Rim and Basin," *Telecommunications Policy* 9, (4) (December), pp. 281–90.

Snow, Marcellus S. and Meheroo Jussawalla. 1989. "Deregulatory Trends in OECD Countries." In *Information Technology and Global Interdependence*, edited by Meheroo Jussawalla, Tadayuki Okuma, and Toshihiro Araki, pp. 21–39. New York: Greenwood Press.

Stern, Robert M. and Bernard M. Hoekman. 1988. "Conceptual Issues Relating to Services in the International Economy." In *Trade and Investment in Services in the Asia-Pacific Region*, edited by Chung H. Lee and Seiji Naya, pp. 7–25. Boulder, CO: Westview Press.

Theus, Dana. 1989. "WATTC and GATT: Help or Hindrance?" In *Proceedings: Pacific Telecommunications Council Eleventh Annual Conference*, edited by L. S. Harms and Dan Wedemeyer, pp. 114–15. Honolulu: Pacific Telecommunications Council.

8

United States-Japan Telecommunications Conflict: Role of Sociocultural Factors

Joseph Doherty

A June 1990 poll conducted in both the United States and Japan indicates that broadening negative popular sentiment in both countries vis-à-vis the other coexists with the rising critical tone in ongoing United States-Japan trade negotiations (*New York Times*, July 10, 1990). The percentage of both U.S. and Japanese citizens polled on overall friendly feelings toward the other country has risen slightly since January 1990 — to 75 percent among U.S. citizens and 66 percent among Japanese. However, responses to other questions indicate that these generally positive feelings hide deep-rooted anxieties on both sides. By 58 percent to 26 percent, Americans now view the economic power of Japan as a greater threat to U.S. security than the military power of the former Soviet Union. Further, 64 percent of U.S. citizens now say that investments by the Japanese in the United States pose a greater threat to U.S. economic independence than European investments. However, the book value of European investments in the United States in 1987 was at least eight and one-half times greater than that of the Japanese (U.S. Department of Commerce, Survey of Current Business, August 1988). When asked to identify their country's strongest competitor, 58 percent of U.S. citizens picked Japan. Almost four in ten U.S. citizens view Japanese companies as competing unfairly with U.S. companies. One in four Americans expressed protectionist sentiments, saying that the United States should restrict Japanese goods a great deal.

Polling analysts reviewing the results found that the increasing anxieties in the United States, particularly those regarding economics, and the bad feelings in both countries were based on largely cultural grounds. Perhaps because of the high visibility of recent

Japanese acquisitions in the United States, such as, the Exxon Building at Rockefeller Center; Citicorp Center, the Mobil Building, and Tiffany Building in New York; and the Beverly Hilton Hotel and Pebble Beach Golf Course in California, 61 percent of the U.S. citizens interviewed in the poll now favor restricting foreign investments in U.S. real estate.

Among the Japanese respondents to the same survey, seven of ten thought the United States looked down on them, and 68 percent feel that the United States blames Japan for its own economic problems. Although 57 percent of the Japanese picked the United States as Japan's strongest competitor, only 3 percent said they thought Japan should restrict U.S. goods a great deal.

Deep-seated anxiety and bad feelings, even latent anger, has surfaced in various ways in both countries. U.S. television advertisements last winter by Chrysler Corporation, featuring its chairman, Lee Iacocca, complained that U.S-made cars were of the same quality as their Japanese counterparts. Comparing specific Chrysler product attributes to the Japanese standard of manufacturing excellence, the ads were objective. A Boone Pickens newspaper advertisement run nationwide on September 18, 1991, was a tough, but objective, attack on the unfair business practices of Japan's powerful corporate cartels (keiretsu). Other U.S. television commercials and newspaper ads, however, featured ominous references to the late Emperor Hirohito and Samurai warriors and ridiculed the Japanese physique, evoking images of nationalism — even racism — in their attacks on Japanese culture.

Congress, leading the fight to open Japan's markets to U.S. goods, has also, on occasion, resorted to symbolic acts. U.S. television viewers remember vividly the image of some U.S. congressmen destroying Japanese products with sledgehammers on the U.S. Capitol lawn. Although President Bush believes that the multilateral General Agreement on Tariffs and Trade (GATT) negotiations are the best forum for opening borders to foreign products, at the February 6, 1989 swearing in ceremony of Carla Hill as U.S. Trade Representative (USTR), he handed her a crowbar, symbolic for applying a little muscle in prying open particularly stubborn foreign markets (*New York Times Magazine*, June 10, 1990).

Growing negative sentiment among the Japanese public is also receiving attention in Japan's media. One of Japan's increasingly popular early morning television programs, Daybreak, focuses on foreign news, with most of its feature stories about the United States. This is not unusual because Japanese life since World War II has been suffused with U.S. culture. Daybreak's coverage of the United States used to be positive and gave insights into the many interesting aspects of life in the United States that was unusual to the Japanese, for example, racial harmony among U.S. sports' professionals.

Indicative of the shifting attitudes of the Japanese toward the United States, however, programs recently have concentrated on U.S. problems such as crime, drugs, corruption, and greed. Increasingly, the image portrayed on the program is one of the United States as a country in trouble, or worse, a society with less culture and less civilization (*International Herald Tribune*, August 8, 1990).

Currently the United States-Japan trade conflict is over such issues as continuing trade imbalances, the problems U.S. firms have in penetrating the Japanese market in specific industries, such as telecommunications, and the differing business structures according to which their respective economies work. These factors, until now, have occupied mainly those government ministries and businesses that were directly involved in both countries. New factors and new dimensions to the conflict have suddenly emerged. Now the citizens of both countries are getting involved. The issues are no longer confined to just economics and trade, but include national security, national esteem, culture, and race. The term "culture," used in the sense of each country's unique socioeconomic structure and its role in the development of United States-Japan bilateral trade problems, has been under negotiation in the context of the Structural Impediments Initiative (SII) since late 1989. SII was introduced as a way of improving the Japanese distribution system, thereby increasing Japan's imports of U.S. manufactures, particularly in computers, satellites, and other telecommunications equipment. Thus pressure created when the USTR named Japan as one of the three countries guilty of unfair trading practices in the Super 301 Clause of the Omnibus Trade Act of 1988 would be diverted (Jussawalla 1990). However, the term "culture" is now used in a different sense. Culture now refers to a people's inner self — its national identity — and is becoming a target of public attack, which increasingly exerts influence on the outcome of the negotiations.

This chapter attempts to bring into focus sociocultural factors and their potential impact on the United States-Japan trade conflict. Because I will analyze only specific aspects of certain sociocultural factors in Japanese society as they relate to Japan's socioeconomic structures, I will draw principally from a few representative Japanese sources in order to gain a Japanese perspective as to its society's future global and domestic needs. A deeper understanding of the sociocultural factors and their impact on socioeconomic structures and economic growth potential may help negotiators and policymakers of both countries in the common tasks that lie ahead.

JAPANESE PERSPECTIVE ON JAPAN'S
FUTURE GLOBAL NEEDS

Generally, in the future Japan needs to:

maintain and expand foreign market shares for its export-oriented economy;

position itself for the newly emerged third science–technology-based industrial revolution;

respond to its new leadership role as a surplus nation in overseas development assistance (ODA);

respond to the changes in the global political-security order; and

attain recognition of its unique cultural contribution to the global community.

Specifically, Japan's future international needs include:

POLITICAL

that the United States retains its global political leadership (toward this goal, the United States must maintain its economic power); and to overcome its deficits (budget, trade, and private sector assets), U.S. industrial production capacity needs revitalization, toward which goal Japan is ready to offer support in terms of the transfer of production technology and production management;

that the United States retains its political leadership of the trilateral system (Japan will need U.S. assistance against possible future protectionist moves on the part of the European Community (EC) after 1992 [compare the article on France's Industrial Shogun, *New York Times*, Business Section, September 16, 1990]);

the strengthening of international organizations — GATT, the Organization for Economic Coordination and Development (OECD), and the International Monetary Fund (IMF) — as a barrier to protectionism and as a mechanism for Japan in carrying out its ODA role;

a stronger international role of the Asian newly industrialized countries (NICs) (Japan is ready to support the addition of the Asian NICs to the trilateral system; looking to support needed capital and technological transfers in boosting the production capacities of Asian NICs in accordance with Japanese domestic demand and in a way that will attract Japanese private sector investments; and looking to ease the pressure building on the U.S. trade deficit from the export-dependent [59 percent] Asian NICs of Hong Kong, Singapore, and Taiwan, opening Japanese markets as well to the primary goods of the Association of Southeast Asian Nations).

ECONOMIC

economic policy coordination with the United States and the
EC: macroeconomic measures with regard to finance and
budgeting; industrial adjustments; and avoiding abrupt
fluctuations in currency markets and interest rates and,
concomitantly, the increasing exchange rate risks that
render plant and research and development investments
unproductive (whereas the role of finance is to fund
economic activity, exchange rates have become divorced
from economic fundamentals; because the world currency
system is international public property, Japan sees the need
to introduce either fixed rates or a system in which member
nations share the costs of maintaining currency stability);
and

increased economic exchange with the United States:
Japanese direct investment in the United States in the
form of production capital and technology in order to make
up for decreasing U.S. investments in expanding its
production capacity, presently running at 81 percent,
thereby aiding the United States in meeting increased
export demand; on the basis of the United States'
superiority both in research and development, for example,
science and technology data bases, scientific publications,
and patents sold to foreign countries, and its service sector
applications in banking, insurance, advertising, and
accounting (the U.S. service sector income ran a surplus in
1988, whereas Japan and West Germany ran a deficit),
Japan looks to an increase of U.S. service sector exports to
Japan;

in its shift from a capital-intensive to a technology-intensive
economy, Japan seeks an international division of labor in
which Asian NICs and the United States would concentrate
on production capacity, and Japan, as headquarters country, would concentrate on capital formation and research
and development.

To fulfill its ODA role:

Japan has to increase public capital flows to less developed
countries (LDCs), increasing its ODA from its present 0.29
percent of gross national product (GNP) to at least the
OECD average of 0.35 percent.

Japan's ODA public capital flows should be in the form of
preparing a viable investment environment, including an
expansion of risk insurance, to encourage a recycling of its
private sector surplus of $30 billion.

In line with the preference of LDCs for aid linked with trade, Japan's ODA measures should concentrate on actual economic, rather than financial, assistance (with its debt obligations) by transferring technology to local industries, especially those in Latin America, to improve employment there and avoid a decrease in per capita income; protecting intellectual property, within the GATT framework, and seeking flexibility of rules regarding the same vis-à-vis LDCs; seeking LDC initiatives in relaxing domestic restrictions on foreign investments; offering tax exemptions and tax deductions to encourage foreign participation in the debt to debenture policy; providing industrial expertise and service information on development policy planning and project design (with regard to project design, Japan itself needs assistance in acquiring ODA know-how, that is, training its personnel and finding analytical tools for development policy planning and project design).

Generally, on the security level, the former global security system based upon political leadership backed by military power, both of which were employed in support of economic and cultural predominance, has broken down. The emerging global order, based principally on economic and cultural leadership, will bring added global political and security responsibilities. This shift has been aided through changes in global perceptions, over the past decades, of national borders from that of territorial hegemony to one of mutual permeation of economy and culture. The future global security system will be based on international solidarity and economic interdependence, with economic and cultural exchanges needed to create a healthy political climate. Bilateral relations will have to be open subsystems within the context of strong international organizations such as GATT, the OECD, and the IMF.

Specifically, Japan's security needs in a threefold context are:

Global: The two military superpowers have found themselves forced to reduce the financial burdens of maintaining a balance of power. The United States may reduce forces in Asia while Soviet conventional forces in Asia remain strong. With European security needs distancing themselves from dependence on the United States, Japan will have to increase its share of global security burdens, participate in economic sanctions, tighten its controls on dual-use technology, and reconsider its pacifist political stance.

Asian Stability: Through increased economic cooperation in terms of assistance, trade, and investment (Japan's recent Assistance for International Development plan), Japan must contribute to the region's stability, offsetting the risks inherent in the region's cultural, ethnic, and ideological diversity.

Third World Stability: Regional conflicts engendered by economic stability threaten the security of global resources, for example, Middle East Oil. Third World economic stability calls for increased economic cooperation between developed countries and LDCs. In assuming ODA leadership, Japan's responsibilities in developing policies combining aid, trade, and investment will increase.

In essence, Japan's security in the future will be based on global economic interdependence and cultural linkage. On the cultural level, as with all of Japan's other above-mentioned international needs, Japan's need for international recognition of its unique cultural contribution will be fulfilled only in relation to Japan's success in achieving the needed domestic changes required by the changing global environment.

JAPAN'S FUTURE DOMESTIC NEEDS

To reach its international goals in a newly emerging global order, Japan must simultaneously achieve certain fundamental domestic transformations.

Sociopolitical

Japan must transform its former technical, economic, and cultural catch-up-to-the-West mentality to one of responsible, creative leadership. Domestically, this will require a transformation from a single-track, government-led, centralized system of ideas and strategies generation, assessment, and dissemination, to a multitrack framework of independent regional and sector input, exchange, and actualization of innovative sociopolitical reforms. New forms of social communication, such as information access, and information evaluation and categorization will be required.

Because Japan's future interests lie in the international community, Japan can only achieve its international goals through an internal internationalization of its domestic society. Japan can no longer afford to be inactive and then be pressured by the United States and Europe into liberalizing its economic structures. The economic structures are only the beginning. Japan must simultaneously internationalize its institutions in all sectors, its customs, and its culture. Only in today's international context can the distinctive Japanese character and cultural contribution sharpen its profile and thus gain esteem.

The catch-up mentality has dominated Japan's political, economic, and social environment since the Meiji Restoration, when Japan's roving ambassadors brought back Western scientific ideas and technological innovations. Since then, however, Japan's modernization has been directed from the top down by interconnected socially elite families in politics, business, and the government bureaucracy. Japan's overreliance on government-led initiatives — that all resources must first be centralized before being reallocated and that all development input-output must first be channeled through government mechanisms, for example, taxes, public funds, budget allocations, and ministry regulations — tends to inhibit the functioning of market mechanisms and stifle creativity.

Japan needs to reform its central government mechanisms to diversify budgeting and resource allocation patterns. More fundamentally than just mechanisms, Japan also needs to reform central government itself, that is, it needs to establish a federal system granting greater authority to local governments to ease the transfer of government functions and institutions, for example, research centers and universities, to localities outside the capital. Further, a reform of the tax and financial systems is urgent: new incentives for promoting new risk ventures and the relocation away from Tokyo, especially of tertiary industries in the finance, information, service, and software sectors are needed now. New advances in telecommunications technology now make such shifts more feasible and cost-effective.

Criticism is based on Japan's emphasis on business-oriented infrastructure, that is, public investments in roads, harbors, airports, trains, and communication, to the detriment of socially oriented public investments in housing, social welfare, sanitation, ecology, leisure, and so on. Japan's government and industry elite have traditionally emphasized the social utility of industrial products as the vehicle for improving Japan's standard of living. Like Germany, Japan favors corporate forms of social goal setting while retaining the efficiencies of the marketplace.

Emphasis is placed not only on improving urban infrastructure in areas such as transportation, sanitation, and ecology to ease the stress on city dwellers but also on the economic advantages of regional infrastructural improvements, for example, in telecommunications, to the geographic integration potential for businesses to (re-)locate, affecting a wider population distribution.

When discussing increasing infrastructural needs, however, Japanese experts have begun to give top priority to improving Japan's research and development capabilities as the future form of social capital required to consolidate the foundations of a new society positioned to meet the global challenge while preserving Japan's domestic economic base. Yet, research and development costs have so grown that not only individual researchers in science and engineering but also the smallest and the largest of Japan's firms are unable to meet the costs. Thus, Japanese experts recommend that their government concentrate on a long-term policy where market mechanisms do not suffice.

However, this necessarily implies that initiatives again come from the top down and will require increased cooperation in the future among Japan's ministries and big business. This approach is not unlike the call in the United States for a national industrial policy to provide public support of major research ventures, such as Semitech (Hollerman 1988).

Do contradictory perspectives clash here? The Japanese realize that their future competitive position in the global economy is based on their research and development capabilities and, thus, given the costs, on top-down centralized government ministerial initiatives. As we will detail later, research and development capabilities can only produce the desired results in an open social environment where individual researchers are challenged to work toward new creative ideas.

Half the equation, then, rests on bottom-up initiatives among diverse individuals and groups within Japanese society. Juxtaposed to the difficulty of finding a public consensus on industrial policy in the United States, we might wonder how difficult it will be for the Japanese not to reach a top-down initiated consensus on research and development policy and other related institutional, regional, infrastructural, and regulatory reforms.

The answers to these questions are related to the type and degree of changes — including the sociopolitical changes — going on within Japanese society today. With regard to changing infrastructural needs and the increasing diversification of desires expressed among different segments of the Japanese population, Japanese experts refer to increasing demands with regard to housing, land, and information versatility; to social benefits related to health care, care of the aging, and the ecological environment; to free time versus working hours; and to income distribution in the face of rising living costs. The increasing demand for culture reflected in the mammoth success in Tokyo recently of museum sales of art objects priced within the reach of the average Japanese came as a surprise to Japanese officials (*Frankfurter Allgemeine Zeitung*, October 26, 1990).

A shift in infrastructure allocations from business-oriented to social-oriented public investments occurs only when broad-based political pressure exists from the populace, that is, from the bottom up. In Japan, such a policy shift cannot be expected to come from the top down, but rather from the bottom up, that is, from newly emerging grass-roots movements. The ruling Liberal Democratic

Party (LDP), the opposing Japan Socialist Party (JSP), and the powerful Ministry of Finance (given its resistance to foreign pressure aimed at changing basic fiscal policies, for example, the U.S. demands in the ongoing SII talks that Japan devote greater resources to infrastructure) are unable to effect such a policy shift.

Regarding such fundamental changes in Japanese society, one study from a leading policy research institute points to recent shifts in Japan's post-war domestic network of social alliances (Utagawa 1990a). One major example is the sudden emergence of the loose coalition of Japanese housewives. Emerging as the largest voting block in Japan's domestic politics, women have a newly discovered political clout that not only signals how drastically different Japan's political environment has become over the past year and the opening of a new era of potentially new alliances in Japan's political arena but also how superficial the notion is that all Japanese move in step to a consensus dictated from above. Women voters are presently concerned primarily with issues close to home, for example, the 3 percent consumption tax, but, with the trend toward increasing telecommunications and information networks including households, women's exposure to more diversified viewpoints and broader issues will most likely increase.

Socioeconomic

In its internal economic internationalization, Japan has already launched initiatives to open its financial bonds and securities markets to foreign financial institutions and its capital markets to non-Japanese resident investors. Japan, too, supports the search efforts for international rules regarding the jurisdiction over multinational corporations' (MNCs) activities. Foreign shareholders will influence Japanese business style: management's emphasis on long-term versus short-term planning, lifelong job security for employees of elite firms, and company loyalty. Japanese business people and investors are learning the social, political, security, and cultural perspectives of its partner countries; the problems relating to the Japanese emphasis of market share over production costs; the symbolic value people place on real estate; and the lack of competitive bidding on public works — buying within corporate groups or even illegal collusion.

Japanese ministry officials have already begun to reflect on the motivation behind Japanese companies' overseas investment expansion. In addition to gainig market shares, securing supplies, and avoiding exchange rate risks, domestic structural constraints, such as higher corporate taxes, land prices, commodity prices, wage and salary costs, and government regulations and restrictions, have become compelling inducements in favor of increased overseas expansion. The domestic side effects — employment gaps, regional economic stagnation, and the destabilization of subcontracting companies — have given ministry officials good reason to consider reforming the tax and industrial regulatory system as a necessary step to preserving Japan's domestic economic base.

However, more fundamental to Japan's economic future is the internationalization of its institutions in related social sectors. Simply adding foreign and nonbusiness members to a company's board of directors is insufficient. Research information has become an economic asset, research and development a basic strategic weapon. The leading edge of research today, however, occurs only in an open international exchange environment. New communication technologies underlying international data flows lie at the heart of the exchange. Eastern Europe has learned its lesson the hard, economic way.

Leading figures from various sectors have called for a reassessment of the functional impact of import regulations. Increasing imports, it is argued, is one way of stimulating domestic demand and domestic markets.

Within the present context of Japan's crumbling internal social harmony, can the Japanese reach a consensus on easing import regulations and, more fundamentally, on restructuring their economic system — finance, production, and distribution? The major ministries involved — the Ministry of International Trade and Industry and the Finance Ministry — are basically in favor of liberalization, but only if it is introduced at a slow pace and in a way that does not intrude on their own areas of competence. Big business, too, supports a similar approach, that is, liberalization is good so long as it does not directly affect their individual industry's special interests. Diet members of the major political parties, along with the labor unions, oppose liberalization when it comes to defending their special interest groups. Other domestic political blocks with few ties to vested interest groups, such as the housewives, are indifferent to such foreign policy–linked domestic issues, as the lack of debate of the same in the most recent lower house elections indicates (Utagawa 1990a).

Given the increasing fractional splintering in Japanese society, chances of reaching a national consensus on such major issues appear to be unlikely and growing weaker as internal diversity mounts. Economic arguments that the Japanese consumer would be the major benefactor of such liberalization policies do not seem to count. That the central problems appear to be related less to purely economic factors than to domestic socioeconomic, sociopolitical, and sociocultural issues are indicated by the emergence of certain focal points centered on the domestic debate.

The issue of rice imports is a good example. Japan's public consensus opposing rice imports has held strong over the past two decades, even though the Japanese consumer pays six times the world market price for his homegrown rice. As recently as 1988, a poll showed that 50 percent of the population was opposed to rice imports. Less than two years later, however, a May 1990 poll revealed that almost 75 percent of the Japanese were in favor of rice imports. Such a quick turnaround — in Japanese, *tenko*, the swift embrace of the opposite point of view — reflects less a shift of public opinion on foreign policy issues, than purely domestic concerns. Housewives, again proving to be a major factor, found the rice prices too high (Utagawa 1990b). The turnaround also showed that the outward appearance of Japanese social harmony, cloaked under the mantle of "consensus," is nothing but a working agreement attained by long behind-the-scenes give and take among groups holding widely divergent points of view. Further, as the shifting alliances within Japan's political landscape presently reveal, Japanese society is neither purely homogeneous nor purely hierarchical in its structure and functioning. Japan's socioeconomic structure is a good case in point.

On the global economic stage, Japan's MNCs have gained international respect, even awe, for their superior production technology and management and the corporate esprit de corps underlying management-labor cooperation. It is easy to overlook Japan's MNCs employing only 30 percent of the Japanese work force. A large proportion of the other 70 percent work in the myriad assortment of small supplier and distributor firms that constitute the underlying support structure of Japan's domestic economy. Employees in these firms, to which employees of Japan's elite firms turn upon retirement at age 55, receive less salary and less benefits and enjoy less job security than do those at major corporations. In an economic downturn, these smaller firms act as shock absorbers to Japan's economic locomotives in weathering the storm.

Both small firms and large corporations, however, share a common perspective: that the household as a business serves as the basic entrepreneurial unit. Traditionally, the small firm often resembles what U.S. citizens refer to as mom and pop shops. The wife is often as engaged as her husband in running the business, especially if the husband's tasks involve travel. A young, promising male worker in the firm, or in a nearby firm, may be a prime candidate for son-in-law, that is, for priming as future head of the household firm. In fact, from the perspective of the household, his becoming a son-in-law in the family is secondary to his legal adoption, which is noted in the household registry. The household as the basic entrepreneurial unit is one of the two rungs on the ladder of socioeconomic mobility in Japanese society.

Analogously, education as the major means of socioeconomic mobility in Japan today, is best understood within Japan's traditional household as socioeconomic unit framework. The main task of the wife, be it in the small firm or in the case when the husband works in a major corporation, is to see to it that the children, especially the sons, excel in school in order to be admitted to the household of elite universities and, upon graduation, to the household of elite corporations and ministries. One of the essential differences between the micro- and macrolevel entrepreneurial households, is that the macrolevel, as a vehicle of socioeconomic mobility appropriately termed the old-boy network, has been closed to Japanese women. Otherwise, the household as basic socioeconomic unit offers a broader social security context than just financially, yet also demands the total dedication of its members, that is, employees to the household, long working hours, and company loyalty. Because, from the Japanese perspective, the household spans generations, management has employee support in its long-term approach to business strategy planning, and the household orientation provides a strong incentive to increased savings.

In today's rapidly changing world, however, Japanese leaders perceive the limitations as well as the advantages of their present domestic socioeconomic, sociopolitical, and sociocultural structures. Global as well as domestic trends in interrelated sectors — economic, political, and social — call for new forms of mobility in all three areas. As in every society around the world, the central question among Japan's elite is how to integrate what is distinctively creative in Japanese society with changes called for in today's global interdependence among nations.

Japanese history reveals that, beginning with the Chinese character script in the fourth century A.D. and Buddhist influences through Korea in the sixth century A.D., the Japanese have again and again been receptive to culturally foreign influences while steadfastly maintaining their own traditional social framework as the foundation for innovative change. Experience has taught them that at critical junctures in their history, impetus coming from other domestic regional areas is essential, for example, as the feudal system centered in EDO, Tokyo declined during the Meiji Restoration period, and strong influences from the Western provinces played a major role in establishing a new social order. The Japanese have also learned that influences stemming from an influx of culturally exogenous ideas can work to their advantage. In its flexible adaptation to standards that are international in nature, Japan profited from new scientific and technical ideas in the Meiji Restoration, from political and legal ideas after World War II, and from economic ideas, for example, on tax system and capital formation, in the 1950s and 1960s. Thus, many Japanese leaders are convinced that by opening the windows of its society to breezes from the newly emerging international climate, its own populace will be more open to necessary domestic reforms. In this context, by easing import regulations, for example, on rice, and benefiting from the internal improvement it brings to the consumer, that is, dropping the price of rice to one-half or even one-third of its present cost, and pulling down prices of other items along with it, the public may agree to not only open other markets, for example, communications, construction, liquor, and tobacco, but also to make other needed institutional reforms such as business practices or the distribution system. In fact, innovations in one sector, such as telecommunications technology and information processing systems, and changes in another sector, such as an increased emphasis on individual choice, responsibility, and flexibility, have reciprocal effects on one another.

Technological breakthroughs in microelectronics have led to the development of sophisticated information processing systems, which, in turn, have brought about advances in production and management methods. These advances have then led to new products and even whole new industries. Coupled with new advances in telecommunications technologies — from audiovisual equipment to modems to home satellite dishes — the new evolving information networks are becoming available to wider audiences. Independent of related government intentions in many countries, advances in communication and information technologies during the past decade have had a democratizing effect on societies all over the world.

When such networks include households, the general public has access to a broad spectrum and huge volume of information pertaining to many different sectors in society. The public then has a wide range to select from, be it on self-help health maintenance measures to ordering meals by fax from different ethnic specialty restaurants in the neighborhood. Diversifying demand, individualistic tastes, greater sophistication, and international flavor affect prevailing attitudes and sensibilities. New customer needs create new markets for new industries producing new appealing merchandise and fashion designs in food, clothing, household furnishings, cars, and so on. The result is changing individual lifestyles, changing social structures, and related changes in business structures as companies attempt to grasp the distribution level of consumer needs; the vertical coordination of production, design, and distribution; and new supply system efficiency to meet new consumer demand.

Japan needs research and development institutional reform of its seniority system and life-long job security, allowing for mobility of talent and flexible use of funding; a more competitive environment; an interdisciplinary approach; multitrack mechanisms for value assessments; a system that is not one-dimensional, that is, run from the top down, surviving only on government allocations, but one that can attract private sector funding, domestic and foreign — one to which the world will look. What Japan needs is a joint research consortium among Japanese industry, academia, and government. Better yet, such a Japanese consortium could be linked with a similar U.S. institution.

Creative minds, however, do not develop after people start working. Japanese leaders realize that new social structures must be forged in every sector, structures that foster greater human freedom and individual attitudes. Japan's educational system is highly efficient. Its high school students score well in international competition but produce less Nobel prizes. Having clawed their way through the school and exam system to reach the leisure reflection afforded in the university atmosphere, is it too late to expect that students will develop intellectual curiosity? School drills are important but are they sufficient to awaken creative talent and encourage its unfolding? New information networks and processing systems are alone insufficient to make the difference. More than ever, students require both logical and linguistic tools for sifting through, ordering, categorizing, and reworking the vast volumes and broad spectrum of information available, as well as a solid grounding in their own sociopolitical, socioeconomic, and sociocultural history as a framework of social perception in which creative minds can flourish.

Japanese leaders are convinced that Japanese society needs and is ready for a new big dose of exogenous ideas, goods, and people to awaken, stir, and challenge the endogenous ideas that are uniquely Japanese. In today's global climate, every country is faced with an intercultural environment that new telecommunications technologies bring into every individual's home and work place.

Sociocultural

Shifts in Japan's post-war domestic sociopolitical alliances is not unsettling to Japanese leaders. Such shifts, based on 180-degree shifts in points of view, are not unfamiliar to the Japanese. What has aroused the attention of Japanese observers is the quickening pace of such shifts over the past year (Utagawa 1990b).

If we look for the cause behind such a sudden move, then the foreign impact through ever-increasing avenues of communication come to mind. Japanese interest in acquiring foreign goods — from French wines to German BMWs to U.S. baseball players to French Impressionist paintings — has developed into a passion.

Japanese society on the social level must shift: from group orientation to individual initiative and self-expression, from intolerance to flexibility, from isolation to coexistence with other races, values, and ideas.

Needed changes in social perception, vis-à-vis two special socio-demographic groups, the younger generation, and the elderly, merit closer consideration.

Values to be fostered within the younger generation include the search for new lifestyles; the need for a more creative environment; a wider range of choices and models in education, for example, interdisciplinary studies; the opportunity for students to adopt new promising ideas, carry them out on their own, and thus meet their own needs; a diversification of facilities in communication; and the promotion of business ventures in design and fashion in the economy.

The elderly need to find greater opportunities for them to put their knowledge and experience to work in the economic and social spheres; to enjoy financial security — an untapped market; to have access to medical treatment and health maintenance; to experience better protection services; to be afforded greater employment opportunities, for example, through reform of the retirement age at elite firms; and to receive a fair allocation of social costs among generations.

Such anticipated changes reflect the underlying changes in social perception already occurring in Japanese society. The most important changes relate to perceptions of the household as the basic socioeconomic unit and related changes in perception of the community and of individuality.

The old-boy network, which binds graduates of elite universities who have gone on to leading positions in business and the ministries, is the only restricted form of the traditional social perception of the household. Individual women who have publicly accused leaders of the old-boy network of abuse and thus have contributed to their downfall are perhaps only a symbol of the potential cleavage between traditional partners in the household as basic socioeconomic unit. The political directions that may emerge out from the spontaneously evolving housewives voting block will be interesting to watch. Returning to the traditional form of the household symbolized in the mom and pop shop is not possible. The modern form, however, could perhaps be more innovative in expressing traditional socioeconomic interrelationships in new ways. Simply dropping members from the household does not appear to be that creative.

Another point of consideration in the changing perceptions of the household is the growing elderly population and the social perceptions of different sociodemographic groups as to the elderly becoming a "burden" on society. The Japanese society is known for its respect of the elderly and its pride in having the highest longevity rate in the world. After years of dedication to the elite company, the retiree also seems to be abruptly dropped from the household and is left with reduced social benefits.

Japan's social net has traditionally been tied to the household. The family form, in turn, has evolved from the predominant form of household at the time. With the separation of work from the family in the elite company household, the company member, once retired, has no adequate social net on which to fall. The same appears to be true for former members of other Japanese household forms, for example, war veterans. Today, the elite company household seems to provide the perspective from which infrastructural development is perceived, for example, corporate housing for member employees, medical care, and leisure time activities. Family needs are only served indirectly. In this context, care of the aged, nursery schools, and youth centers are not provided. The legal system can also be viewed in the context of the elite household in which the ministries are empowered by laws enacted by the Diet to resolve conflicts, for example, with firms on ecological problems; in the United States, such power is entrusted to the courts.

Japanese leaders attempting to meet society's changing needs are quick to point out that the Japanese should be careful to retain the good in their cultural tradition and to build the new national spirit upon their existing cultural essence and view of life.

With shifts in social perception regarding the household as the basic socioeconomic unit, we might also expect related shifts in people's perceptions of more fundamental aspects of the Japanese social framework, for example, space, distance, time spans, the "atmospheric," with related shifts in the Japanese conception of the self and its expressions in language. Such shifts in social perception might be expected to have repercussions on existing social interrelationships and interactions among both various sectors and sociodemographic groups.

Traditionally, the Japanese perception of the self has been oriented primarily in relation to others. The Japanese people perceive themselves first and foremost as social beings, independent but incomplete in themselves, as members of multiple concentric social rings. The individual has varying degrees of development, attaining selfhood, or maturity, which is the process of acquiring the correct judgment for a particular situation as to the proper balance between individual aspirations and social requirements. Adherence to social constraints, learning to restrain one's feelings and self-expression, and making efforts on behalf of a particular circle (for example, the performance of one's role, such as working long hours), are perceived as fostering individual development and building individual character. Learning that human beings are fundamentally interdependent lies at the core of Japanese upbringing.

Although all points on the circumstance of each circle are equidistant from their common center, distances between points on different concentric rings are highly differentiated. Members of a particular circle, for example, a household (*ie*) perceive clearly defined tangents at every point on the circle delineating outside or out in front behavior, ceremony, formality, or appearance (*omote*), on the one hand. On the other hand, inside behavior — behind the scenes activity — is the appropriate social framework in response to outward social constraints (*giri*) on the circle members, for example, outward consensus in business negotiations. Behind the scenes setting (*ura*) is appropriate to personal emotional expression (*ninjo*), for example, prior lively discussion and disagreement among members of the firm's negotiating team.

This outside or inside axis is observable as the spatial framework in every social setting and situation on every social level from the smallest household to one of the largest households, for example, the industrial federation Keidanren. Language parallels the spatial dimensions of social life: the use of personal pronouns only to clarify a situation, the adjective verb, informal verbal, situation-centered archaic Japanese-coined Chinese characters (*kanji*), which have been indispensable to Japan's modernization process, that is, to late nineteenth century Meiji intellectuals in assimilating Western technical terms in science, technology, and philosophy.

Group organization evolves, in part, within this spatial social perception axis. The authority of the group leader (the head of the household) derives from the circle members, informal and equi-distant (egalitarian), where everyone in the group has input at a business group discussion meeting, as in socializing after work. From this perspective, Japanese management is employee oriented. To misuse authority would be to drive a wedge through the circle. Authority is also perceived as representative of the circle. If something goes wrong with even one member of the circle, the circle representative takes responsibility for saving the honor of the circle. One example is the recent resignation of the chairman of Sumitomo, Japan's third largest bank. From this perspective, we can also understand why, when a JAL jumbo jet crashed a decade ago, the JAL chairman personally offered apologies to the victims' families.

The other axis in social perception is the time dimension. Whereas the concentric rings appear to spread out as waves in chronological sequence from the center, when viewed from the horizontal plane, from a point high enough above the vertical axis, every point on each circle appears to be equidistant. Within every Japanese household on every level, the members' social perception framework includes not only an entrepreneurial but also a religious dimension, that is, the presence of the sacred in the form of the ancestors. This perception is carried over as the pyramidal (hierarchical) dimension in every group organization. Social perception is that age — seniority based on experience both within a household and among one (the older, more experienced firm) — carries with it a certain respect and prestige. This is why the business card is so important in Japan. Time as presence of the sacred within the household provides the basic social perspective of the depth of every situation. To experience this requires training, prereflective thought of the world, the air, and the situational atmosphere (*ki*) in which members find themselves together, interdependent from others before the subject-object split (Kimura 1969).

For the Japanese, with their affinity to Zen, this atmospheric *ki* is the stimulator of genuine creation in the arts, culture, and thought. This experience of the depth of each situation, with many potentially conflicting meanings involved, carries into the Japanese preference for leaving interpersonal situations ambiguous. Yes and no responses, especially from one who is exercising authority derived from the circle members, would reveal a lack of consideration, which is one of the highest virtues in life. This ambiguity underlies the apparent cleavages in Japanese society between inside and outside, real intention and official opinion, and social customs and law. In Japan, real intention (*honee*) sometimes wins out over law, for example, in business bargaining, which to Western perception seems to reveal as untruth.

Are there subtle shifts going on in present-day Japan regarding this basic social perception framework and its embodiment in social structures? Has the separation between work and family in the elite company household had an impact on the traditional Japanese perception of the egalité of the role performance/careers of its members — male and female — on the circle. That is, are women, who receive less salary and less benefits, who are assigned less challenging work than they are qualified for through their education, and who enjoy less job security even perceived as being household members on the egalitarian circle? With the quickening tempo of technological innovation, the faster pace of changing consumer products and attitudes, the lightening speed of information accessibility, and the available entertainment distractions, is the vertical time dimension, the awareness of presence and atmosphere, fading from social perception? Because of the increasing demands of entrance exams, business competition, and women's dual roles as education mama and second breadwinner in the family (women constitute 40 percent of the work force), has the delicate outside/inside balancing act between adherence to social constraints and individual aspirations become too stressful to an ever greater number of Japanese?

According to the previously mentioned list of domestic needs to fuel a creative society, a research and development–led economy, and a populace open to global currents, such shifts in social perception seem welcome if not essential. To meet its emerging role as a world leader, Japan requires greater individual initiatives and self-expression, fast-track lanes for younger creative talent, and more diversified communication facilities accessible to ever broader household audiences offering an ever wider range of choices.

As in countries in other regions of the world, Japan appears to have no alternative other than to open its society further to international influences. As other countries have experienced, Japan, too, faces increasing internal social disruption. Despite the strength of Japan's economy, many Japanese leaders are worried about a widening of the domestic employment gap, a continued weakening of the regional economies, and further destabilization of the subcontracting companies and mom and pop shops. Japanese observers are concerned about the further breakdown of existing sociopolitical alliances, what political direction newly emerging blocks such as the "housewives" will adopt, and whether extreme political groups will gain greater sympathy among voters.

Political trends are rooted in a society's customs and values. How extreme political movements develop is related to the degree of disruption of the social perception framework. In such a case, the populace encounters difficulty either in finding their way in handling their daily problems — the children receiving a proper education, the grandmother needing special care, a woman being denied promotion at an elite firm and seeking legal redress — or in discovering their society's values and social priorities reflected in present social practices and in the exercise of sector competence. In either case, an increasing percentage of the population may experience problems relating to their cultural identity. It is in such a vacuum that extreme groups, right and left, offer simplified, ideological solutions to those looking for something to hang onto as an emotional substitute.

Current trends in Japan do not indicate such levels of sociocultural disorientation. Urban housewives from rural backgrounds still maintain sufficient concrete ties to their past roots — the ratio of Japanese households that earn part of their income from farming rose to 70 percent in the 1980s — so that their judgment on rural-related issues is not about to be based on purely bucolic notions. There are also no alarming indications that the Japanese voting populace is about to swing radically to the left, despite the fact that the opposition has gained control of the upper Diet House.

Somewhat disturbing to observers, however, are the recent undertones voiced about Japan's pacifism and its involvement in its own security in Shintaro Ishihara's best-seller, *The Japan That Can Say No.*

Mounting international responsibilities are befalling Japan because of its economic superpower status, therefore, it is not surprising that, when faced with the increasing pace in the shift in domestic social alliances, the Japanese people are slowly beginning to direct their questions outward to their post-war external alliances.

According to many Japanese experts, the growing United States-Japan conflict is not based principally on economic questions. Issues such as Japan's economic system, business practices, and industry protectionism, especially toward high-technology products and rice, it is argued, have little impact on imbalances but are political and cultural in nature (Utagawa 1990a). Japanese leaders agree that Japan has to liberalize its economy, but to do so the government needs to establish a consensus, and, given its politically weakened condition, that takes time. The Japanese public is traditionally inward-looking and has only begun to recognize the international problems and responsibilities that their country's economic success has brought them. This is one reason why Japanese leaders see the urgent need for a big increase in domestic telecommunications capacities and diverse information networks in order to increase the exposure of Japanese households to global currents in every field.

To open Japan's markets calls for fundamental changes in Japan's socioeconomic and sociocultural structures. With Japan's internal social alliances undergoing deep shifts, thus, weakening the country's political leadership, the Japanese elite is searching for ways to quicken the process of social change without destabilizing Japanese society to the degree that would invite extreme political elements. One possible approach, already in progress, is to encourage movement from the bottom up, for example, the formation of new voting blocks, such as the housewives. Appropriate measures that government leaders could take would be to increase information to the public on global issues and Japan's role therein. Such measures support the Japanese leaders' views of expanding telecommunications capacities, also of consumer households, as a basis for developing a more creative research and development–based economy.

In today's world of global communication, cultural isolation is no longer an option for any nation. International interdependence, however, takes place not among globally neutral individuals but among peoples from distinct sociopolitical, socioeconomic, and sociocultural backgrounds. On the one hand, Japan urgently wants and needs international input in opening its society and modernizing further, that is, adapting its socioeconomic and sociocultural structures to international standards. On the other hand, Japan also seeks international recognition as a center of creativity, both economically, for example, in research and development, and culturally. Through the country's internal internationalization, Japanese leaders hope to round off Japanese society's rough edges, refine its national character, and present itself as a nation of integrity to the world. There is also perhaps a slight missionary touch in presenting an alternative model to those of the two superpowers in a rapidly shifting global political arena in which ethnic and cultural diversity is becoming a key issue. A new movement to counter the economic-dominated world reports of the World Bank and other international organizations has surfaced within the United Nations Educational, Scientific, and Cultural Organization, calling for the publication of a world culture report. Given the nationalistic trends in Eastern Europe, the former Soviet Union, and elsewhere, observers are concerned whether culture could also become an ideological weapon for peoples forced for decades into a remnant sector corner.

Japanese leaders welcome external pressure (*gaiatsu*). Ever since Admiral Perry sailed into Tokyo harbor in 1853, forcing the Meiji Restoration, Japanese policymakers have used external pressure as a domestic political tool in forming a public consensus on liberalization measures. As experience with the development process in LDCs over the past four decades has taught, however, outside pressure is only effective to the degree that the populace, not just the government, is prepared to respond. The populace's response, in turn, is determined almost solely by the internal situation, particularly the level of internal sociocultural (dis-)orientation and the related ideological level. In Japan, where despite shifting social alliances, disorientation and ideological levels remain low, insofar as foreign pressure concentrates on single concrete issues (for example, cellular telephones) chances of the leadership achieving a public consensus, given sufficient time, are good. Even on issues that have seemingly strong cultural connotations, for example, rice imports — where rice is a main staple in the Japanese diet with even spiritual overtones — shifts in public consensus, earlier assumed unattainable, are possible. Business experience reveals that if a firm's product is competitively superior, people everywhere will buy it despite their opposition to the country of origin. In cases, however, that go beyond single concrete issues to matters of changing socioeconomic structures, for example, reducing a particular ministry's range of competencies, then the ministry will attempt to place stumbling blocks in the way of the consensus-building process. The Japanese Ministry of Agriculture, for example, with little remaining in the area of competence, attempted to raise the national debate on the liberalization of rice imports to the ideological level by introducing the national security factor — the danger to securing Japan's food supplies.

Other social organizations, however, such as the Buddhist-backed Clean Government Party, the big business federation Keidanren, and the general populace, kept the debate centered on the practical issues.

Changes on the sociopolitical, socioeconomic, and sociocultural levels are always possible, but they only come when society itself realizes that there is no other alternative given the path society has selected. At the same time, changes must evolve out of the society's own sociocultural perspectives if the disorientation level and the concomitant ideological level are to be kept low.

Sociocultural factors are fairly insensitive to normal fluctuations in society, namely, those in the economic and political sectors. Once, however, sociocultural disorientation begins to mount in a society, that is, when an ever-larger percentage of the populace perceives itself as being backed into a remnant sector corner, then ethnic, religious, or culturally based ideological levels can rise in nonlinear fashion. Social change is essential in the modernization process. Internally it may be disconcerting, especially to entrenched interest groups. But so long as social movement is able to exercise itself in practical areas — education, communication, health care, law, and the economy — it must sooner or later prove its efficiency and efficacy, for example, as a good educational institution, to gain the acknowledgment of the public it claims to serve. In an increasingly global community, cultural diversity and diverse innovative approaches also spur overall growth. Each society's output in every sector, from politics to economy, from education to health care, from communication to culture, is acknowledged and respected, not for its ethnic, racial, or religious origin, but for the unique quality of its contribution to the human community.

CONCLUSION

In negotiations on the United States-Japan telecommunications conflict, the United States should continue to use its two-pronged approach in pressuring Japan: its piecemeal approach to specific industry-related trade markets, for example, satellites, and its broader economic approach to structural issues, for example, public sector investments in telecommunications. Both approaches fit well with the Japanese government ministries' use of pressure as a tool in building a domestic consensus on liberalization measures.

In selecting negotiation topics, further consideration should be given to the interrelationships between the two approaches. First, in what areas is the United States presently ahead in the telecommunications field among products, services, and research and development? Second, what are Japan's most urgent domestic sociopolitical, socioeconomic, and sociocultural priorities, and viewed from these perspectives, what are Japan's most pressing domestic needs?

Japan's most pressing domestic needs are the real target of the negotiations on SII, which has touched on issues far beyond the announced changes sought after in both countries' economies. For example, Japanese proposals that the U.S. government limit the number of credit cards U.S. consumers can hold, which is viewed economically as a way of curbing U.S. consumer spending, that is, increasing U.S. savings — has an effect on more than just a form of legal tender or personal credit rating. It symbolizes further the holder's social status (blue, gold, or platinum), the individual's freedom, and his personal integrity. The facial expression of the hotel desk clerk or car rental employee, vis-à-vis an individual who does not present a credit card, leaves no doubt in a customer's mind that he is considered untrustworthy at best, although the Japanese term for outsider or foreigner (*gaijin*) would be more appropriate. Not just credit card companies, but all U.S. citizens find such a proposal to be an attack on the U.S. way of life, suggesting that both sides should exercise restraint in proposing reforms that the other country should adopt.

Because both sides are willing to permit such sensitive issues to be put on the table is both unique and promising. As the deputy USTR, S. Linn Williams, said, "We have never attempted anything like this before. These are two sovereign countries, big countries, that are discussing issues that until now were considered no one's business but their own. At times, the talks ventured into areas so rooted in national culture that they seemed sure to fail" (*New York Times*, June 29, 1990).

Opening discussions on such structural issues by the Japanese was perhaps even more impressive. Among the many fundamental changes that the Japanese negotiators agreed to were those touching on the Japanese household enterprise at different levels. First, Japan agreed to the liberalization of a law virtually protecting small mom and pop retail household shopkeepers from competition from large Japanese, and U.S., retail chains offering discount and foreign goods.

Most interesting perhaps was the public support that U.S. negotiators received from Japanese consumers who welcomed U.S. pressure as a tool to press their own demands for lower prices on consumer goods, housing, etc. This consumer trend is backed by the *New York Times*/CBS News/Tokyo Broadcasting System Poll cited previously. In response to the question Why has the United States not sold more goods in Japan?, 48 percent of the Japanese cite Japanese import restrictions, and only 35 percent cite the poor quality of U.S. goods. The figures are almost precisely reversed from those of a 1987 poll. Those who agreed that Japanese companies were competing unfairly rose, too, between the two polls, from 16 percent to 26 percent. Changing attitudes in Japan reflect a recognition that many of the U.S. demands for more open markets and internal reforms of the Japanese economy would actually benefit Japanese consumers. It also reflects a reduction in the general population's recognition of the significance of problems facing the United States-Japan relationship. Within Japan's shifting social alliances, bottom-up initiatives are starting to get results. The Japanese government also committed itself to strengthening consumer protection through measures allowing Japan's Fair Trade Commission to assist consumers who seek legal redress against unfair business practices.

Although it demonstrates how flexible Japanese society can be in accepting foreign ideas, such consumer support conceals the difficulties each side faces in finding a consensus among their own respective constituencies on the agreed issues. U.S. lawmakers in Congress tempered their positive reactions with a "wait and see" attitude about Japanese enforcement of their side of the agreement. Same day editions of the *Mainichi Shimbun*, one of Japan's leading newspapers, echoed Japanese doubts as to whether curbing consumer spending in the United States was not only politically unpopular but also "an impossible thing anyway." At the same time, each side consented to put such issues on the table, indicating that each government sees hope of obtaining a public consensus. The traditionally cautious Japanese ministry officials usually do not extend themselves. They even seem more willing these days to make public the inside, behind-the-scenes disagreements between ministries. U.S. government officials may sense also that the U.S. public may be willing to tighten their collective credit belt in order to help balance the budget.

Monitoring the enforcement of the agreement and taking the hard trade results is important. Besides watching the economic indicators, social indicators may also be helpful in assessing medium- and long-term trends that could exert input on when and what impact this strategy will achieve. The numbers of young researchers in research and development management positions might serve as one socioeconomic indicator of shifts in socioeconomic mobility in Japan; so, too, might the number of women in management positions in elite household companies and organizations. The number of younger employees of elite firms who have switched companies within the past year would serve as a indicator, not only of changing attitudes toward company loyalty but also of changing social perceptions among the younger generation of the traditional Japanese time dimension. Older persons living in institutions might serve as an indicator of changes in the social perception of the relationship between the household and the family.

Sociopolitically, polls of ranking issues that concern housewives might serve as an indicator of the trend in bottom-up initiatives and their direction in the context of shifting social alliances. Other sociopolitical indicators might include the number of litigation cases brought by women and retirees against elite corporate households.

The copies sold of best-sellers on national issues from ideological perspectives might serve as one sociocultural early warning indicator of shifting trends toward either end of the social spectrum. Other sociocultural indicators, for example, might include the number of youth participating in household rituals honoring their ancestors; the ratio of suicides among retirees from elite corporate versus nonelite business households; and the divorce ratio of families related to elite corporate versus nonelite business households. Socio-demographic categories could be expanded to include new potential trend-setting groups, such as women (Utagawa 1990a). Analysis of the correlations among microlevel social and political indicators and the macrolevel economic indicators would also help in assessing trends.

Negotiators on both sides have made steady progress on individual issues, particularly in the telecommunications sector. Their success in the SII negotiations could even be termed remarkable, considering the fundamental changes in their respective socioeconomic structures, which they have set as their goal.

Success in the SII negotiations may help both sides in reaching piecemeal agreements on industry-specific issues. Making the Japanese distribution system more competitive, for example, should help increase imports of U.S. goods, such as computers and other telecommunications equipment. In the area of telecommunications equipment, the United States has already succeeded in obtaining a breakthrough on two issues that were long a subject of dispute: supercomputers and communication satellites. Further, at the beginning of August 1989, the Japanese agreed to remove barriers blocking U.S. companies from selling network channel terminating equipment — a device allowing signals from business equipment such as computers to be transmitted over telephone lines — directly to customers. In telecommunications services, progress is also being made. The August 1989 agreement also removed barriers blocking U.S. companies from offering telephone services such as voice mail and electronic banking. In one area of basic applied telecommunications technologies, the United States gained an important victory when, in June 1990, the Japanese Ministry of Post and Telecommunications selected the software controlling the vital digital transmission component using computerized radio pulses in cellular phones designed by Motorola as the nationwide technical standard for its next generation of cellular telephones. This software can carry three times the calls of present analog technology. Motorola's victory over other competitors, including Japan's giant Nippon Telegraph and Telephone (NTT), which provides almost all local and long-distance phone service and most of the cellular service in Japan, may not bring short-term financial gain to Motorola. However, it is one example — another is Motorola's digital voice encoder, a vital component that will convert the wave pattern of a human voice into a pattern of pulses in future cellular telephone handsets — showing the U.S. edge in areas that will bring long-term advantages.

In this context, it appears questionable that the United States adopted a consumer-oriented perspective in negotiations over Japan's increasing its public sector infrastructure investments in bridges, airports, ports, roads, sewage plants, parks, and public housing. The theory was that the Japanese, when living in bigger houses, driving on wider roads, etc., would also become greater consumers of foreign goods. In the short term, this may help close Japan's savings and investment gap and help certain U.S. sectors, such as construction, and the Japanese consumer. But in the long term, which becomes ever shorter in the fast-moving technological revolution, U.S. superiority in basic applied technologies would seem to support the adoption of a different perspective. The Japanese agreed to spend the amount the United States set, but not to the desired fixed percentage. Instead, they added another $100 billion through recently privatized companies such as NTT. Under this privatization the Ministry of Posts and Telecommunications retained 90 percent of NTT.

SII offers to both countries a framework for approaching the task of coordinating the measures and tools required in fostering their respective domestic industries: the orderly decline of old industries and the buildup of high-value-added industries of the future. In this context, both sides are progressing in the same direction, sharing mutual interests. Future economic growth lies in research and development, where the United States is superior and where Japan places its future hopes. One great SII success was the U.S. commitment to increase spending for scientific and commercial research and the Japanese pledge to reduce the time it takes to issue patents. Without using the tabooed term, U.S. negotiators in the SII, with Japanese encouragement, took a big step toward formulating an industrial policy for dealing with the present economic problems and future economic needs of both countries.

The negotiators realize, perhaps better than anyone else, that despite their success in reaching the SII agreement, the process of resolving the trade conflict has just begun. It appears that Japanese negotiators may even have acted prematurely by presenting a consensus outwardly before having reached one inside their society. The next step of implementing the agreements, that is, forming a consensus on the needed measures among their respective ministries and constituencies, will be much tougher, especially if pressure or negative popular sentiment, driven by worsening economic reports, continues to rise.

In Japan, comic books (*manga*) often appear more directed at adults than children; economic, political, and pornographic comic series are published. As elsewhere in free societies around the world, comic strip writers enjoy a certain literary freedom in handling topics and expressing thoughts otherwise left unsaid in society. One comic series, published by Kodansha, a major publisher in Japan, is entitled "The Silent Service" (*Frankfurter Allgemeine Zeitung*, October 15, 1990). The story is about Japan's role in today's quickly shifting global politics. With U.S. help, Japan has secretly built a new nuclear-driven submarine. During a test run, the submarine commander revolts against both his Japanese and U.S. superiors and escapes. The United States intends to sink *Yamato* in order to prevent the new technology from falling into Soviet hands. In ensuing naval battles, first the United States and then the Soviet Union suffer heavy losses. The pressure of fast-moving events forces the Japanese government to side with the mutineer, while the United States and Soviet Union conclude a secret pact to destroy *Yamato*. The Europeans, at first hesitant, join with the United States and Soviet Union. Official Japanese efforts to reach a peaceful solution fail. Japan and the United States declare war on one another. Both fleets are headed on a collision course near Okinawa.

The trade negotiators and ministries of both countries still have a long, hard, zigzag course to maneuver.

REFERENCES

Hollerman, L. 1988. *Japan Disincorporated: The Economic Liberalization Process.* Stanford: Stanford University Press.

Jussawalla, Meheroo. 1990. "Challenges for Trade in Telecommunications." Paper presented to Intercom Conference, Vancouver, October.

Kimura, B. 1969. "Zur Wesensfrage der Schizophrenie im Licht der japanischen Sprache" *Jb. Psychol. Psychother. u. Med. Anthropol.* Vol. 7.

Powell, J. 1989. *The Gnomes of Tokyo: The Positive Impact of Foreign Investment in North America.* New York: American Management Association.

Utagawa, Reizo. 1990a. "The Weathering United States-Japan Relationship: A Perspective from Japan." Policy Paper. Tokyo: International Institute of Global Peace.

___. 1990b. "Japan: Rice Import Issue." *Washington Post*, June 7.

9

Application of Game Theory to United States-Japan Trade Friction in Telecommunications

Meheroo Jussawalla and Yale Braunstein

Events of December 1990 at the General Agreement on Tariffs and Trade (GATT) proved the triumph of bilateralism over multilateral free trade. The collapse of the GATT talks at Brussels and the inability of negotiators to resolve their differences brought to light the unwillingness on the part of member countries to give up protectionism in its overt or covert guises. Although farm subsidies were considered as the villain of the piece, the effects of the breakdown of the Uruguay Round spread havoc in the area of trade in services. According to the United Nations Conference on Trade and Development data, trade in information services is growing at 16 percent per year and reached $165 billion by the end of 1991. Total services trade is reckoned at $600 billion.

GATT has held seven trade liberalization rounds since its inception. These rounds have created an aura around GATT as being the only international regime that fostered prosperity through trade. But the GATT regime has been weakened by regionalism that emerged with such agreements as the Enterprise of the Americas Initiative and the agreements between the United States and Canada, the United States and Israel, and the United States and Mexico. These agreements have taken precedence over multilateral free trade to the extent of involving fast-track approvals on the part of the U.S. Congress. While Article 24 of GATT's constitution does permit free-trade customs unions, its main mission is to promote multilateral efficiency in trade through an efficient global division of labor. Regional and bilateral trade can and does readily divert trade and thereby redirects global resources from efficient allocation.

Both the United States and Japan are playing leading roles in the expansion of telecommunications technology and services and will continue to do so. Competition between them has led to a consumer boom such as has never been witnessed before. In the vibrant Pacific region, both countries play a prominent part in setting the patterns of telecommunications usage and in the introduction of intelligent systems. Japan's gross national product (GNP) is already in the region of $4 trillion, which is twice that of Germany. Japan is home to eight of the world's ten largest public companies and boasts seven of the world's largest banks. Along with Japan, the Asian newly industrialized economies (NIEs) constitute a critical marketplace for trade. These countries represent the United States' seventh largest trading partner, even as the United States represents their second largest, Japan being the first.

Historically speaking, the current United States-Japan conflict has no precedent. Japan has always remained in the orbit of the Western world in international relations. With nationalistic pressures growing on both sides, the greatest challenge for the leaders of both countries is to combine their strengths in economic terms and in the pursuit of democratic values. Emmott (1989) points out that high savings and skilled approaches to production, trade, and finance have enabled Japan to achieve impressive economic success. The U.S. savings and investment gap is being filled by the rest of the world. A great deal of misapprehension and dissension has emerged on both sides without concrete changes being made toward improved relations in telecommunications trade or market penetration. Although it may be true to some extent that the U.S. military depends on Japan's electronic devices and semiconductors, as claimed by Ishihara (1989), the changes in Eastern Europe and the demand for telestroika clearly indicate that threats of selling computer chips to Russia will be counterproductive in an environment of better global relations. The United States-Japan trade conflict was triggered by the refusal of the Japanese Ministry of Posts and Telecommunications (MPT) to permit Motorola to sell its cellular telephones in Tokyo city. This event was followed by the naming of Japan as one of three countries by the U.S. Trade Representative (USTR) in the Super 301 Clause of the Omnibus Trade Act of 1986. If protectionist trade policies were the sole cause of Japanese success, then India, Brazil, and Argentina, who are far more protectionist, would now be among the world's richest countries. The Structural Impediments Initiative (SII) started at the close of 1989 has been a way of diverting the pressure created by the Super 301 Clause action. It aims, among other goals, to conduct a joint study to improve the Japanese distribution system and thereby increase Japan's imports of U.S. manufactures, particularly in computers, satellites, and other telecommunications equipment, along with forest products.

This chapter will first examine the background of conventional trade theory as it applies to telecommunications trade between the United States and Japan. The details of the SII and the mergers within the industry will also be discussed in order to build a case for the application of game theory to the moves and countermoves of both countries in specific telecommunications industries and trade policies affecting their output. We will examine the differences in the regulatory policies of the two countries as they affect trade in telecommunications along with the regulatory framework being discussed at GATT. Next, an alternative view will be introduced of the trade friction between the two countries on the basis of a game-theory approach. Finally, we will discuss the role of the services trade negotiations in GATT and the telecommunications annex proposed by the United States. The issue of an emerging consensus between the two trading partners will be addressed.

TRADE THEORY AS APPLIED TO UNITED STATES-JAPAN TELECOMMUNICATIONS TRADE

Trade theory based on comparative advantage did not cover trade in services, which was considered to be intermediate rather than final goods. Telecommunications technology has altered that concept, and information services are traded as final products. In current trade flows, goods and services related to information are among the most dynamic sectors of the trade between Japan and the United States. Any restrictions in the form of tariff and nontariff barriers cause friction between the trading partners. Flows of data accompanying trade are important in this relationship because they deal with information about markets, product descriptions, technical data, and information about the general framework of trade and monetary policies.

Conventional theory based on factor intensity and factor availability did not take into account nonmarketable flows of information that take place within a firm, such as communication between the headquarters and subsidiaries of transnational corporations (TNCs). Even marketable flows of information are invisible and difficult to evaluate and locate physically. Another dimension of current trade practice that differs from received theory is that a substantial part of services trade takes the form of direct foreign investment (DFI) as part of the operations of TNCs in their merger and joint venture activities. These actions are considered to be attempts to reduce the transaction costs of exporting services. It is difficult to separate the production of trade in services from their consumption, and DFI becomes a means of selling services in foreign markets.

The question of market access for services also defies trade theory inasmuch as information access in trade gets restricted, thus becoming a difficult issue in trade relations (Aranson and Cowhey 1988). It has culminated in the naming of Japan under the provisions of the Super 301 Clause of the U.S. Omnibus Trade Act of 1986. So far the United States has outperformed all other nations in the services sector, but if world trade now slows down many developed and developing countries will become vulnerable to trade losses. Traditional trade theories have been replaced by strategies for market access: DFI and nontariff barriers such as voluntary restraints and quotas. The failure of the Cairns Group to save the GATT negotiations in December 1990 illustrates the strength of the protectionist lobby within its 107 member countries.

Global markets today are influenced by political and social systems and by TNCs that intervene in the competitive pricing of traded goods and services. Trade theory had stipulated that when specialization combined with laissez-faire the results would be an equalization of factor prices and an elimination of the differences in factors incomes between trading countries. While this theory explained the patterns of trade, it omitted the effect of such dynamic variables as technical change emerging from inputs of knowledge and information. Services trade is directly influenced by information technology and its impact on economic growth. Comparative cost ratios are only an indirect response to price changes and cannot explain trade in information services. Imports of information affect the gains from trade in their impact on productivity within the importing country. When competition among producers exists for marketing information-intensive products, it gives rise to a demand lag for information-related imports. The lag occurs because although trade theory factors in transportation costs, it fails to include information costs in calculating the balance of trade. In the real world we find that services trade is likely to increase as the services sectors of major trading countries grow in volume and value. For example, Japan's services sector in 1990 accounted for 63 percent of its GNP compared with 57 percent in Germany, 63 percent in the United Kingdom, and 71 percent in the United States. The telecommunication services alone are funnelling $79 billion a year into Japan's total output.

Another deviation from trade theory is the hypothesis that factor accumulation leads to a deterioration in the terms of trade for the commodity that uses the accumulating factor intensively. This hypothesis does not consider the impact of technology on information as the accumulating factor. Demand for the hardware of information technology (such as computers, semiconductor chips, satellites, and mobile telephones) is increasingly price inelastic, thus neutralizing the negative effects of imports on the importing country's GNP.

The import penetration ratio in information-intensive products for the Pacific region is determined not just by exports from Japan and the United States but by supplies now flowing from Korea, Taiwan, Hong Kong, and other countries. New and diverse forms of wealth are being created, which alter conventional trade policies. Japan's import penetration ratio is estimated to rise from 5 percent in 1988 to 10 percent in 1995 (*The Economist*, December 17, 1988).

Telecommunications Trade Issues and the Structural Impediments Initiative

The trade gap between the United States and Japan remained at $50 billion for several years so that in November 1989 an unprecedented round of trade talks commenced between trade officials of the two countries to address the root causes of the trade imbalance. It was felt that trade practices in three technologically advanced sectors of the Japanese market were protectionist, namely, microprocessors, super-computers, and satellite hardware. (Added to these were forest products with which we are not dealing in this book.) At this time, the Ministry of International Trade and Industry (MITI) announced a plan for buying U.S. products and offered $1 billion worth of tax credits to companies that boosted their U.S. imports by 10 percent. Even so, political anxiety was mounting over trade relations resulting in revisionist lobbies within the U.S. Congress demanding protectionist trade policies. So far the United States has eliminated its trade deficit with Europe and reduced it with other countries; therefore, the Japanese surplus continues to be a highly visible and contentious problem. Added to this problem was the impression that Japan's contribution of $13 billion to the Gulf war was paid only after intense U.S. political pressure. Japan is now an economic superpower, and the world's expectations for Japan are commensurate with its achievements.

Another protectionist issue that is closely linked with the telecommunications networks has surfaced between the two countries. It is proposed that automated global trading of financial futures start very soon. A computerized trading system called GLOBEX, jointly developed by the Chicago mercantile Exchange and Reuters, involves trading interest rate and currency futures and contracts during the 16 hours that the Chicago exchange remains closed. GLOBEX is already linked to New York, London, and Paris exchanges and accounts for three-fifths of all financial futures traded on the world's exchanges. Japan's Ministry of Finance has refused permission to such Japanese financial institutions as Mitsui Trust and Banking to install GLOBEX terminals. In Japan, as in the United States, a legal barrier separates banking and securities industries, but the countries differ in implementation. It may take a long time before this problem can be resolved to permit global trade in financial futures emanating from Japan. Meanwhile, U.S. investment companies are effectively prevented from participating in the Japanese financial futures market.

In early April 1990, the two countries faced deadlines on at least a dozen trade agreements. An interim report on deep-rooted structural barriers to U.S. imports, such as Japan's distribution system and high prices, was submitted to both governments. As part of the SII, satellites, semiconductors, and super-computers have become crucial components of the trade conflict between the two countries. MITI is earmarking $1.5 billion in loans to importers and $1.5 billion for a data bank that will link foreign exporters with Japanese importers. Tariffs will also end for 1,000 items this year. These measures could reduce the trade conflict between the two countries by an appreciable extent, depending on the response by Japanese companies. While the SII talks and the GATT Round may help to some degree in reducing the tension, they cannot compensate for the shortcomings of U.S. macroeconomic policies. Japanese negotiators at the SII talks already have expressed concern over the low saving rate in the United States, the continued budget deficit, and the low levels of worker training programs. Some actions in these regards would strengthen the hands of U.S. negotiators in penetrating foreign markets. The International Monetary Fund, in its *World Economic Outlook* for 1990, has called attention to the macroeconomic imbalances in the U.S. economy and suggests that any attempts to deal with it through trade policies would be ineffective. Countries are also apprehensive of the unilateral action that the USTR is taking through the Super 301 to stem unfair trade practices. This action goes against the GATT code for multilateral negotiations. Concern in Washington, D.C., grows as Japan accounts for 60 percent of the U.S. total trade deficit.

One factor inhibiting the reduction of the trade surplus in Japan is that exporters to Japan face powerful alliances of corporations, such as Mitsui, Mitsubishi, Sumitomo, Fuji, Sanwa, and Dai-Ichi Kangyo, each with its own banks, retailers, and real estate. These are the *keiretsu* that permit fixing prices and sharing the market among themselves. In most cases, antitrust laws in the United States do not allow similar collaborations. With their *keiretsu* organization, Japanese manufacturers maintain high domestic prices and support a distribution system with 1.6 million retailers.

The MITI plan may not spur imports from the United States also because in accounting there is a fundamental relationship between trade balances and investment gaps. The difference between a country's exports and imports must exactly equal the difference between its saving and investment (Feldstein 1990). Because the MITI plan does not alter the savings and investment propensities of the Japanese, it is not likely to reduce their exports. It is also possible that the plan would increase imports from Japanese subsidiaries abroad rather than from U.S. exporters. Finally, the U.S. dollar continues to be overvalued in terms of the yen. If we consider that over the past three years the wholesale prices of tradeable goods in the United States have risen by 13 percent, the real exchange rate of the dollar is higher that its nominal rate. Thus the possibility that the MITI plan will succeed at expanding U.S. imports without an appreciation in the value of the yen to keep pace with the inflation in the United States and the stable prices in Japan is not very likely.

As far back as 1985, U.S. trade policy vis-à-vis Japan set its sights on the goal of reducing Japan's savings rate in order to close the bilateral trade gap. According to the Economic Planning Agency of Japan, the average Japanese household saved 15.1 percent of its income in 1987 (*Japan Times*, November 1, 1989). In 1989, household savings aggregated to ¥10 million. In contrast, the U.S. saving rate for the same year was 6.6 percent. The Maekawa Commission in 1987 recommended that Japan should eliminate its incentives for savings, such as tax exemptions. Accordingly, Japan abolished the maruyu tax-free status of saving. But this did not end the trade friction between the two countries. Japan's latest import promotion plan subsidized by MITI may help to reduce the trade gap if the large exporting and trading houses follow the rules. But, as indicated above, if the Japanese plan fails to change either the rate of savings or the total Japanese investment, it will not reduce the trade surplus it now enjoys. This trend applies not only to the United States but also to other trading partners of Japan because it now controls one-tenth of the world's total trade.

The trade friction that Japan continues to encounter with the United States and the European Community has complex components, but they mostly amount to differences in corporate cultures. The dispute over semiconductors is a good example of how far rules of international trade are rooted in European values and categories. In April 1987, Ronald Reagan signed a bill imposing 100 percent duty on $300 million worth of Japanese-made goods because of Japan's noncompliance with the United States-Japan Semiconductor Agreement signed in September 1986. By the end of 1988, Japanese dumping had stopped, but because of price inflation the major beneficiaries were the Japanese suppliers because their exports gained from rising U.S. prices. Japan still dominated the dynamic random access memories (DRAM) market. Of the $16 billion semiconductor market in Japan, 90 percent was still supplied by domestic producers. This case demonstrates the ineffectiveness of protectionist policy imposed without industrial restructuring.

When countries attempt to solve a trade dispute bilaterally, GATT does not have any say if the agreement is broken by any one party. As such, both countries will have to solve the problem through multilateral talks at GATT. Technorivalry is at the heart of the dispute.

The U.S. argument is that the Japanese have enjoyed the benefits of latecomer transfer of technology from the United States. But technological reciprocity is not allowed because Japanese research and development is done in corporations that are outside government control. This aspect of technonationalism surfaced when the NEC Corporation of Japan was not permitted by the United States to participate in the U.S. government supported consortium (Sematech) for manufacturing semiconductors.

In February 1990 trade talks between the United States and Japan concentrated mainly on telecommunications, satellites, and supercomputers. The only issue settled under telecommunications seemed to have been the Motorola case. However, in August 1990, after four months of bargaining, the United States and Japan reached an agreement that would open the Japanese market to products and services offered by U.S. companies. These included value-added services such as voice mail, electronic banking, and advanced facsimile transmissions. The agreement also removed barriers preventing direct sales to customers of network channel terminating equipment. The United States had always opposed MPT's policy of regulating type II services suppliers and the sale of digital equipment. Under existing Japanese regulations, virtually all customers served by NTT are required to buy or lease their equipment from NTT. The new agreement will allow customers to purchase from foreign manufacturers, and this should eliminate the control that NTT had over the market control which discriminated against foreign suppliers.

Joint ventures between U.S. and Japanese information technology firms have played a significant role in restructuring corporate assets. U.S. producers have found such mergers to be a low-risk method of cracking global markets. For example, American Telephone and Telegraph (AT&T) struck a deal with NEC in 1990 to trade its computer-aided designs for NEC's advanced logic chips. Likewise, Texas Instruments combined with Kobe Steel to manufacture logic chips in Japan. Motorola has ventures with Toshiba and Hitachi, Intel with NMBS, and Advanced Micro Systems with Sony (see Table 9.1). This spate of joint ventures raises questions about the basic significance of trade barriers and bilateral agreements. On the one side, SII talks were progressing at the government level, and on the other, industries were making their own arrangements bypassing government negotiations. The benefits for the U.S. corporations differ in each alliance. They range from licenses to Japanese technology, involvement in Japanese production of memory chips, or exposure to Japanese manufacturing techniques. Such mergers vindicate the stand taken by Kenichi Ohmae in *Borderless World* that corporations are going global, owing their loyalty to their international customers rather than to their country governments, thereby diffusing trade disputes.

TABLE 9.1
Major Alliances in the Semiconductor Industry

U.S. Company	Japan Company	Year
Texas Instruments	Kobe Steel	1990
AT&T	NEC	1990
Advanced Micro	Sony	1990
AT&T	Mitsubishi	1990
Intel	NMBS	1990
Texas Instruments	Hitachi	1988
Motorola	Toshiba	1986

Source: *Wall Street Journal*, March 20, 1990.

This spate of joint ventures raises questions about U.S. trade policy under which the United States is pushing for a larger share of the Japanese chip market. In October 1990, the U.S. Semiconductor Industry Association (SIA) and the Computer Systems Policy Project (a group made up of 11 leading U.S. computer manufacturers) asked the Bush administration to negotiate a new, five-year agreement with Japan to open its market more to U.S.-made semiconductors. The SIA had originally planned to file another trade complaint against Japan because Japan had fallen short of its agreement to allow the United States a 20 percent share of its semiconductor market. The group took the more moderate course because of recent gains in the Japanese market and the prospects of future gains. However, government and industry officials in Tokyo have previously maintained that a new pact is not needed and have expressed reservations against any new targets for market access.

Regulatory Policies and Technological Rivalry

Technorivalry between the two countries emerged partly because of divergent deregulation of the telecommunications industry. The Telecommunications Business Law of Japan passed in 1985 was expected to open the market to competition from the United States for type II services or value-added, non-basic networks. However, NTT had entered the U.S. data market by establishing data bases and data communications centers in the United States for Japanese companies doing business in the United States. The U.S. market for data services is $40 billion and is growing 20 percent a year. As such, NTT will compete on U.S. soil with firms such as AT&T, General Motors' Electronic Data Systems, and US Sprint.

Deregulation of the U.S. telecommunications industry and the divestiture of AT&T in 1984 served as a model for Japanese policymakers. In 1985, the privatization of NTT started with capitalization of $5.6 billion and the government owning 15.6 million shares.

Two-thirds of these shares should pass into private hands by 1992, but foreigners are not permitted to own any. Currently only 5 million shares are held by private Japanese investors. In 1985 the market oriented sector selective (MOSS) talks were held between the United States and Japan to negotiate the entry of U.S. telecommunications equipment suppliers into the deregulated Japanese market. Japan then amended its Radio Law to allow foreign firms to compete in the cellular telephone market. All tariffs on telephone instruments, telegraph equipment, radio communications equipment, and electronic switches were eliminated at the close of 1986. Deregulation had created an explosive growth of Japan's telephone market. By 1990 there were 50 subscribers per 100 persons and 240,000 subscribers for cellular telephones. For the United States, these figures are approximately 90 telephone subscribers per 1,000 persons and 100 cellular phones per 1,000 subscribers. Three new suppliers in the type I service — Daini Denden, Inc., Japan Telecom Ltd., and Teleway Japan — have offered lower rates than NTT.

Deregulation also gave growth to the satellite services offered since 1989 by two companies: Japan Communications Satellite Company (JC Sat) and Space Communications Corporation. JC Sat has a collaboration agreement with Hughes Communications, and Space Communications has an agreement with Ford Aerospace (now Space Systems/LORAL). In the international communications market Kokusai Denshin Denwa was challenged by International Telecom Japan and by International Digital Communications (IDC). IDC is a joint venture of Cable and Wireless, Toyota, C. Itoh Company, and Pacific Telesis. This conglomerate started in 1989 to lease submarine optical fiber circuits between Japan and Hong Kong, Singapore, the United States, and Canada.

By 1989 NEC had grown to become the world's largest seller of chips, fifth in communications equipment, and fourth in computers. Even so, its sales in 1989 were $21.3 billion — one-third that of IBM and one-half that of AT&T. As Japan moves toward integrated services digital networking by 1995, its purchases of computers and telephones will grow to $5.5 billion. NEC will then benefit from its integration with IBM Japan. NEC is a member of the Sumitomo keiretsu and supplies 30 percent of Japan's home satellite dishes. NEC also competes against Cray Research in the market for super-computers.

The mainframe market is also currently dominated by Japan. Amdahl Corporation, now 50 percent owned by Fujitsu, has announced a new set of mainframe computers that can perform 600 million instructions per second. IBM has also announced similar mainframe capability, although its world share is eroding. But component suppliers in the United States are coming from Korea, Taiwan, and Singapore who are offering competition to Japanese imports.

It is difficult to maintain a vibrant computer industry in the United States without a strong semiconductor base. Japan controls the computer market because it controls the component supplies. Toshiba's goal is to replace all U.S. desktop computers with laptops, Sony entered the market to compete with Sun microsystems, and the imports of Japanese workstations in the United States are showing a sales growth of 34 percent per year. Whereas in Japan both MITI and private industry are pouring funds into computer technology and artificial intelligence, U.S. antitrust laws and lack of tax credits are proving restrictive for the U.S. industry. Already Japan is working on a neurocomputer with neural chips and using optoelectronics. These developments have led the Massachusetts Institute of Technology to establish a research and development center in Japan at the Sakura Science Park (Chiba).

Satellites have the highest value-added component of Japan's high-technology systems. The Japanese goal is to capture 20 percent of the world market, estimated at $25 billion, for space applications by the year 2000. This goal is not aimed at profits, but the strategic importance was proved in the Gulf War. Japan budgeted $1 billion for its space industry in 1990 and is building its unmanned space shuttle (HOPE). However, Japan's space technology is at an early stage of development. As a result, Mitsubishi's Sakura communications satellite costs $195 billion compared with a GE satellite that costs $100 million, including launch costs. Furthermore, launch costs from Kyushu Island are far costlier than Ariane launches from French Guiana or U.S. launches from Florida.

Satellite trade talks with the United States have been at a stalemate for several months. In April 1990 the Japanese government agreed to a compromise by changing its previous stand of indigenous construction of its CS-4 satellite for domestic communications. So far Japan has given infant-industry protection to its satellite industry. The United States refuses to accept this policy because Japan is not a developing country and its development of experimental data-tracking satellite facilities is viewed as a discriminatory trade barrier by the USTR. Japan has already sent a spacecraft called *Hagomoro* into lunar orbit. In 1992 Japan will, in cooperation with the United States, launch the *Geotail* for exploring the earth's magnetic field and has agreed to cooperate with the United States for its space station the future of which has become uncertain. This is still in the planning stage.

GAME-THEORY APPROACHES TO UNITED STATES-JAPAN TRADE FRICTION

Since the 1944 publication of *Theory of Games and Economic Behavior* by von Neumann and Morganstern, the concept of the competitive process has been restructured and presented in terms of games strategy. The assumption of strategic interdependence between or among players is paramount to this theory; in many ways the appeal of the game theory has paralleled economists' increased interest in general, rather than partial, equilibrium. Basically a "game" consists of precise descriptions of the economic agents involved (the "players"), their preferences, the options available to each, and the results arising from their choices from these options. Furthermore, games usually have well-specified rules concerning the order of play and the information available to each player before a move. (There is not complete agreement on what constitutes a game; this list draws on Schotter and Schwodiauer [1980]. Definitions of the terms used in this section can be found in the appendix.)

Games can either require that players act simultaneously or sequentially. In this context, simultaneously does not necessarily mean at the same time; rather, it implies that each player chooses his action before becoming aware of the choices of the other players. Many games consist of a number of rounds of play, each of which is also a game. Given the sequential nature of many games, in a decentralized economy the players in a noncooperative game might make choices that result in situations that are not Pareto optimal. One example of this may well have been the decisions made by the United States in negotiating the Semiconductor Agreement of 1986 with Japan.

One application of game theory is to predict which stable institutional forms will emerge from a given set of economic conditions and what the resulting value relationships will be. For example, the case of United States-Japan trade friction in telecommunications is probably a cooperative, non–zero-sum game. In other words, the negotiators for the two countries may communicate and enter into enforceable agreements, and the motives and outcomes are not strictly antagonistic. The specific nature of the game is to determine how to divide the likely gains from freer trade so that both countries have incentive to form and maintain a coalition.

Looking at some of the solutions to particular games often enables us to understand whether such agreements are likely to emerge. For example, we should like to determine whether the solutions are stable. In the cooperative trade-liberalization game, we determine which imputations are likely to occur and not be eliminated by further bargaining. This leads to the concept of the core of the game — those imputations that are not dominated. It is possible that the core might be empty: objections may be raised by one or another player to all points in the core. By restricting our analysis to the case of justified objections, we eliminate this possibility. The resulting solutions are know as the bargaining set.

Nash Bargaining

We start our formal analysis of United States-Japan telecommunications trade with a model that has a cyclical pattern in the imbalance. The stylized facts are as follows:

First, the United States issues a protest against a specific market restriction by the Japanese.
Next, Japan either denies or justifies the practice.
The United States threatens to retaliate by a specified date.
Bargaining or negotiations occur.

In a majority of the cases, just as the deadline approaches, Japan makes concessions or some other solution emerges. The length of time each move may take and the overall length of the cycle varies, and a number of products and practices may cause the friction. Furthermore, it is possible for more than one cycle to occur concurrently.

Chan (1988) has shown that the Nash bargaining model can easily be adapted to model trade negotiations of this sort. Nash's original work (1953) was axiomatic in nature and lacked a description of the mechanisms that bring about the solution he described. Later research has found such mechanisms (Binmore & Dasgupter 1986), and it is now common to apply the Nash model to a variety of situations if the specific uses are shown to satisfy the necessary assumptions.

Chan (1988, p. 354) uses four assumptions in his general analysis:

1. Players (countries) have full information on the preferences of their opponents (trading partners).
2. In a well-integrated world financial market, countries have identical discount rates.
3. Negotiators from each country have equal bargaining skill.
4. Assessing trade gains is complicated and costly.

Each assumption applies to some degree to the United States-Japan situation. The first assumption is not unrealistic as each country has access to each other's economic data, and public information on political structures and processes is readily available. Also, the two countries meet often to discuss trade and related issues, and in so doing each informs the other about its preferences. This information helps each choose negotiation strategies (courses of action).

At one level the goal of both countries is to maximize some measure of welfare or utility. Specifically, each country can be thought of as seeking to improve its trade balance. This is admittedly simplistic in that it ignores internal debates in both countries, such as whether lower prices for imported agricultural goods reduce self-sufficiency (Japan) or whether certain manufactured items are being sold at below home-market prices (the United States).

The second and third assumptions are necessary to make the analysis symmetric. It is possible that the Japanese take a longer view, and there are a number of stories about the comparative skill of the negotiators from each side.

Comparisons are useful only with respect to each country's individual welfare scale. The more general form of the fourth assumption — the solution is independent of irrelevant alternatives — has been the subject of considerable debate. It simplifies the evaluation process because only those alternatives that result in gains from freer trade need be assessed. But it implies that "the outcome of bargaining, as identified by the solution, . . . depends only on the relationship to the disagreement point and does not depend on the other alternatives in the set" (Roth 1979).

Together these assumptions make the bargaining solution efficient, symmetric, and independent of irrelevant alternatives. It is intriguing to speculate how close they are to describing reality and how any divergences between specific assumptions and reality affect the conclusions of the model. In addition to the points mentioned above, it is possible that the United States will receive more of the gains from freer trade, whereas Japan's primary benefit of trade liberalization is its continued ability to trade with the United States. However, consumer goods are highly priced in Japan, and increased competition in the marketplace should lead to lower prices, which, therefore, benefits the Japanese consumer. (Of course, this ignores the question of whether improved consumer welfare ranks highly in the social welfare function seen by Japan's negotiators.)

The general conclusions emerging from Chan's thesis (1988) would be risk aversion of some traders, reduction in the cost of disagreement, and a less-balanced consumption pattern for one of the trading partners.

These outcomes can be compared with those that would result from free trade. Because free-trade equilibria require only ordinal utility functions, a change in the degree of risk aversion (the marginal rate of utility of income) has no effect on the benefits received by the trading partner. As in the Nash bargaining case, a change in tastes in favor of the abundant commodity of a country reduces trade and lowers the gains of the trading partner.

Applying these conclusions to the United States-Japan negotiations and comparing the Nash bargaining solutions to the free-trade outcomes provide the following insights:

If Japan has a higher degree of aversion toward risk, then the United States will benefit, and vice versa. However with free trade the degree of risk aversion has no effect on the gains of the trading partner.

A change in tastes toward an abundant commodity (for example, domestic consumer goods) will either reduce the cost of disagreement (in the negotiation model) or reduce trade (in the free-trade model). In either case, the gains to the trading partner are reduced. Similar conclusions result from an increase in a scarce commodity (for example, labor in Japan).

Friction Cycles

Although Chan's model provides interesting insights concerning the likely outcomes of trade negotiations, it does not capture the stylized facts of the trade negotiation process. Matsuyama (1990) developed a trade-liberalization model based on a Nash-equilibrium game in which the government and a domestic firm alternate moves. We adapt this model to describe the moves in a friction cycle in general and then apply it to the specific case of denial of bandwidth to Motorola.

We first assume that two countries are in equilibrium; this eliminates the possibility that they are actually at some point in another cycle. The game begins when the United States protests some trade practice of or market condition in Japan. At the beginning of period 1, Japan has the options of correcting or removing the market-restricting practice (C) or not correcting it (NC). If Japan chooses C, the game ends and trade continues on the basis of new post-game conditions. If Japan chooses NC, then the United States must decide whether to retaliate (R) or not retaliate (NR). If the United States chooses R, the game ends and, assuming retaliation takes the form of increased tariffs, Japan loses some of its share of the gains from trade. In this case a different set of post-game conditions exists from those described above. If the United States chooses NR, the game remains at status quo while negotiations take place under the threat of retaliation in a future period. Japan is able to end the game by choosing C in any period prior to the deadline set for retaliation. The maximum number of periods over which the game can take place is, therefore, known to both parties. When this time elapses, the United States will choose R, and the game ends.

Changing notation slightly, we can apply this model directly to the Motorola case. The game began on April 29, 1989, with the United States accusing the Japanese MPT of limiting access for U.S. products and services to the Japanese market for cellular radio-telephone service. The U.S. action followed a complaint from Motorola that Japan was not abiding by part of the 1985 agreement to open its telecommunications market to foreign vendors. Specifically, the

USTR determined that Japan was violating the MOSS agreements on telecommunications in claiming that bandwidth was not available in Tokyo to accommodate the Motorola-made mobile telephones used by the cellular telephone systems established by Daini-Denden, Inc.

Japan had two options immediately following the protest (period 1). It could assign the desired bandwidth (A) or not (NA). If Japan had chosen A, the game would end with trade occurring under new conditions. The United States would have received additional gains from trade, and its current trade balance would improve, *ceteris paribus*. However, Japan chose NA. The United States then had the choice to retaliate (R) or not retaliate (NR). The United States chose R, but it threatened to retaliate (choose R) on July 10, 1989, if Japan did not choose A by that date. Japan continued to have the option of choosing A or NA in each period (day) until the deadline. Negotiations occurred, and Japan chose A on June 29, 1989, thereby avoiding retaliation and ending the game.

In Tables 9.2, 9.3, and 9.4, we show that this model can be used to describe the friction over Motorola's MicroTAC cellular telephone, semiconductor imports, and satellite procurement. In some cases the specific outcomes may change over time. For example, the introduction of new, smaller, and lighter cellular telephones may change the nature of the outcome resulting from strategy pair (II,A) of Table 9.2.

TABLE 9.2
The Case of Motorola's MicroTAC

UNITED STATES
Strategy A
Accept actions taken by the Japanese government; no retaliation or political pressures against Japan.

Strategy B
Accept actions taken by the Japanese government with limited approval; continue to negotiate for further acceptance of U.S. telecommunications equipment and services by the Japanese.

Strategy C
Reject actions taken by the Japanese government; start procedures to apply the Super 301 clause for full retaliation.

JAPAN
Strategy I
Allocate bandwidth to be used by NCC with MicroTAC; allow NCC to operate all over Japan.
  Pair (I,A)
    MicroTAC becomes available all over Japan and will dominate the mobile telephone market at least for a few years.

Table 9.2, continued

Pair (I,B)

MicroTAC becomes available all over Japan and will dominate the mobile telephone market at least for a few years. Further concession by the Japanese government may be expected in telecommunication, but Japanese confidence in the United States will be eroded.

Pair (I,C)

MicroTAC becomes available all over Japan and will dominate the mobile telephone market at least for a few years. Dissatisfaction with the strong U.S. policy will be generated in Japan. Research and development in Japan to develop a portable terminal comparable to MicroTAC will be promoted very strongly.

Strategy II

Allocate bandwidth to be used by NCC with MicroTAC for only a part of Japan that includes the Osaka-Kyoto area, but excludes the Tokyo area.

Pair (II,A)

MicroTAC will become available within the region in which bandwidth is allocated for it and will dominate the mobile telephone market in that region. Users who cannot use MicroTAC will start demanding MPT to approve it in other regions.

Pair (II,B)

MicroTAC will become available within the region in which bandwidth is allocated for it and will dominate the mobile telephone market in that region. Users who cannot use MicroTAC will start demanding MPT to approve it in other regions. Research and development in Japan to develop a portable terminal comparable to MicroTAC will be promoted.

Pair (II,C)

MicroTAC will become available within the region in which bandwidth is allocated for it and will dominate the mobile telephone market in that region. Dissatisfaction with the strong U.S. policy will be generated in Japan. Research and development in Japan to develop a portable terminal comparable to MicroTAC will be promoted very strongly.

Strategy III

Do not allocate bandwidth for MicroTAC; all mobile telephone terminals to be used in Japan are to be manufactured in Japan.

Pair (III,A)

MicroTAC will not be available in Japan. Strong dissatisfaction by U.S. manufacturers will emerge and they will press the U.S. government to pursue some legislative action for retaliation.

Pair (III,B)

MicroTAC will not be available in Japan. Negotiations between the U.S. and Japanese governments will be continued in order to open the Japanese mobile telephone market. Research and development in Japan to develop a portable terminal comparable to MicroTAC will be promoted.

Pair (III,C)

MicroTAC will not be available in Japan. Acute confrontation between the U.S. and Japanese governments will emerge, possibly leading to repeated retaliation, not only in telecommunication but also in other trade. Both the United States and Japan will be losers.

TABLE 9.3
The Case of Semiconductors

UNITED STATES
Strategy A
Accept actions taken by the Japanese government; no retaliation or political pressure is to be exerted on Japan.

Strategy B
Accept actions taken by the Japanese government with limited approval. Continue to watch the share of IC imported from the United States in the total sales of IC in Japan. If it is expected that the share is not going to reach 20 percent, give warning to the Japanese government. Execute limited retaliation by restricting imports of selected commodities from Japan, if the share ends up below 20 percent for a year.

Strategy C
Reject actions taken by the Japanese government; start procedures to apply the 301 clause for full retaliation, if the share ends up below 20 percent for a year.

JAPAN
Strategy I
Accept the "20% requirement" of the U.S. government. Subsidize the major semiconductor manufacturers in Japan for importing IC from the United States; use price subsidization and adjust the subsidy rate so that the share of IC imported from the United States becomes at least 20 percent of the total sales of IC in Japan.
> *Pair (I,A)*
> The share of IC imported from the United States in the total sales of IC in Japan will be maintained at the level of 20 percent. Under the subsidization, the Japanese semiconductor market will be expanded, and the price of IC in Japan will be lower than otherwise.
> *Pair (I,B)*
> Same as pair (I,A).
> *Pair (I,C)*
> Inconceivable pair.

Strategy II
Accept the "20% requirement" of the U.S. government. Make efforts to induce the major semiconductor manufacturers in Japan to import IC from the United States, so that the share of IC imported from the United States increases and becomes close to 20 percent of the total sales of IC in Japan. This is to be done by "moral suasion," without relying on economic or legal measures.
> *Pair (II,A)*
> The share of IC imported from the United States in the total sales of IC in Japan may or may not be maintained at the level of 20 percent. If it is not maintained, dissatisfaction will be generated from U.S. manufacturers of semiconductors.
> *Pair (II,B)*
> The share of IC imported from the United States in the total sales of IC in Japan may or may not be maintained at the level of 20 percent; the share, however, will be higher than the outcome with strategy pair (II,A). If the share is not maintained, U.S. manufacturers of semiconductors will be dissatisfied. Further, when retaliation, even if limited, is executed, dissatisfaction will emerge among the general public of Japan.

Table 9.3, continued

Manufacturers of commodities on which U.S. retaliation is applied will consider it unfair.

Pair (II,C)

The share of IC imported from the United States in the total sales of IC in Japan may or may not be maintained at the level of 20 percent; the share, however, will be higher than the outcome with strategy pair (II,A) or (II,B). If the share is not maintained, U.S. manufacturers of semiconductors will be dissatisfied. Further, when retaliation is executed, dissatisfaction will emerge among the general public of Japan. Manufacturers of commodities on which U.S. retaliation is applied will consider it unfair.

Strategy III

Do not accept the "20% requirement" of the U.S. government. Leave the semiconductor market free to operate by itself.

Pair (III,A)

The share of IC imported from the United States in the total sales of IC in Japan will be less than the level of 20 percent. U.S. manufacturers will express strong feelings of dissatisfaction to the U.S. government and to Japanese semiconductor manufacturers.

Pair (III,B)

The share of IC imported from the United States in the total sales of IC in Japan will be less than the level of 20 percent. U.S. manufacturers will express strong dissatisfaction to Japanese semiconductor manufacturers. Further, when retaliation, even if limited, is executed, dissatisfaction will emerge among Japanese manufacturers of commodities on which the U.S. retaliation is applied.

Pair (III,C)

The share of IC imported from the United States in the total sales of IC in Japan will be less than the level of 20 percent. U.S. manufacturers will express strong dissatisfaction to the Japanese government and to the Japanese semiconductor manufacturers. Further, when retaliation is executed, dissatisfaction will emerge among Japanese manufacturers of commodities on which the U.S. retaliation is applied. An acute confrontation between U.S. and Japanese governments will emerge, possibly leading to repeated retaliation, not only in semiconductors but also in other trade. Both the United States and Japan will be losers.

TABLE 9.4
The Case of Satellites

UNITED STATES
Strategy A
Accept actions taken by the Japanese government; no retaliation or political pressure is to be exerted on Japan.

Strategy B
Accept actions taken by the Japanese government with limited approval. Continue to negotiate, case by case, on the extent to which the Japanese government procure noncompetitively from the manufacturers it chooses.

Strategy C
Reject actions taken by the Japanese government; start procedures to apply the Super 301 clause for full retaliation, if the Japanese government rejects competitive procurement.

JAPAN
Strategy I
Accept the requirement by the U.S. government that the Japanese government procure satellites, including parts and related systems thereof, in the international competitive market whenever they are for commercial use exclusively or partially.

  Pair (I,A)
    Most of the Japanese government's procurement of satellites will be made from U.S. manufacturers because of the technological difference in satellite production between the two countries. The speed with which Japanese manufacturers develop technology for satellite production will slow down considerably and Japan will remain an importer of satellites for the coming decades.
  Pair (I,B)
    Same as pair (I,A).
  Pair (I,C)
    Inconceivable pair.

Strategy II
Accept the requirement to a limited extent: some of the parts of the related systems for a satellite may be purchased from Japanese manufacturers, if the level of their technology is comparable with the technology of U.S. manufacturers. If a satellite is to be used for noncommercial purposes, the Japanese government may procure from noncompetitive Japanese manufacturers.

  Pair (II,A)
    The Japanese government's procurement of satellites will be made competitively from U.S. manufacturers and noncompetitively from Japanese manufacturers. If only a small portion of the procurement is made from U.S. manufacturers, dissatisfaction will be generated in the United States. The speed with which Japanese manufacturers develop technology for satellite production will be faster than in the case of pair (I,A).
  Pair (II,B)
    The Japanese government's procurement of satellites will be made competitively from U.S. manufacturers and noncompetitively from

Table 9.4, continued

Japanese manufacturers. Intense negotiations will take place between the two governments on the extent to which the Japanese government may procure noncompetitively from the manufacturers it chooses. Negotiations may be made in conjunction with issues other than satellite procurement, possibly producing unexpected outcomes. If only a small portion of the procurement is made from U.S. manufacturers, dissatisfaction will be generated in the United States. The speed with which Japanese manufacturers develop technology for satellite production will be faster than in the case of pair (II,A).

Pair (II,C)

The Japanese government's procurement of satellites will be made competitively from U.S. manufacturers and noncompetitively from Japanese manufacturers. The United States will retaliate by applying to the Super 301 clause. The speed with which Japanese manufacturers develop technology for satellite production will be faster than in the case of pair (II,A).

Strategy III

Reject the requirement. The Japanese government will procure satellites, including parts and related systems thereof, from the manufacturers of its choice.

Pair (III,A)

The Japanese government's procurement of satellites will be made competitively from U.S. manufacturers and noncompetitively from Japanese manufacturers. Strong dissatisfaction will be expressed to the U.S. and Japanese governments by the U.S. manufacturers; strong political dissatisfaction with the Japanese government will also be generated in the United States.

Pair (III,B)

Same as pair (III,A).

Pair (III,C)

The Japanese government's procurement of satellites will be made noncompetitively from both U.S. and Japanese manufacturers. Strong dissatisfaction will be expressed to the U.S. and Japanese governments by the U.S. manufacturers; strong political dissatisfaction with the Japanese government will also be generated in the United States. Further, when retaliation is executed, dissatisfaction will emerge among Japanese manufacturers of commodities on which the U.S. retaliation is applied. An acute confrontation between the U.S. and Japanese governments will take place, possibly leading to repeated retaliation on many trade items. Both the United States and Japan will be losers.

Matsuyama's analysis calculated the payoffs to each player and shows the importance of the time preferences of each. (This is the major reason deadlines are part of the negotiation strategies of the players.) Adapting Matsuyama's notation, we have four possible final states of the market:

M: Japan does not correct, and the United States does not retaliate (NC–NR). This is the equilibrium at the start of the game. We define M_J and M_{US} to be the payoffs to Japan and the United States for each period these conditions obtain.

N: Japan corrects before the United States retaliates (C–NR). Trade continues under the revised terms with a greater share of the gains going to the United States. The new one-period payoffs are N_J and N_{US}.

P: Japan does not correct, and the United States retaliates (NC–R). Trade continues under the new condition of retaliatory tariffs. The new one-period payoffs are P_J and P_{US}.

Q: Japan corrects, but after United States retaliation is in place (C–R). This assumes there is a lag before the tariff is removed. The new one-period payoffs are Q_J and Q_{US}.

If we define $0 < d_J < 1$ and $0 < d_{US} < 1$, where d is the discount, to be the discount factors for the two countries, we can calculate the payoffs for both countries at any specific termination point. For example, should Japan choose to correct in period 1, the payoffs are as follows:

to Japan: $N_J + d_J N_J + d_J^2 N_J + ... = N_J / (1 - d_J)$,
to the United States: $N_{US} + d_{US} N_{US} + d_{US}^2 N_{US} + ... = N_{US} / (1 - d_{US})$.

Following the same logic, if Japan waits until period 2 to correct, the payoffs are:

to Japan: $M_J + d_J N_J + d_J^2 N_J + ... = M_J + d_J N_J / (1 - d_J)$,
to the United States: $M_{US} + d_{US} N_{US} + d_{US}^2 N_{US} + ... = M_{US} + d_{US} N_{US} / (1 - d_{US})$

since state M exists for one period and state II exists for the remainder.

Both the Nash bargaining model, as adapted by Chan, and the friction cycle model of trade liberalization developed by Matsuyama describe many of the strategies and outcomes in recent high-technology trade disputes between the United States and Japan. In particular, the outcomes of these trade disputes are often as predicted by the Chan-Nash model. Furthermore, in the Motorola mobile telephone case the specific actions of both the U.S and Japanese negotiations almost perfectly parallel those in the equivalent rounds of the friction cycle model.

MANAGED TRADE VERSUS GATT

If we apply the theory of managed trade proposed by Bagwell and Staiger (1990) to the United States-Japan case in telecommunications equipment, then the United States would benefit from special protection when the trade volume surges without economic harm to Japan. This theory of managed trade is based on the hypothesis that a dramatic increase has occurred in special forms of trade barriers like voluntary export restraints (VERs) and orderly market arrangements. This kind of intervention is referred to as managed trade to characterize current trading arrangements. It refutes the noncooperative Nash equilibrium view as being inadequate to explain low baseline level of protection in certain sectors of exports and imports. Self-enforcing agreements or tacit cooperation among countries is assumed for managed trade. Dixit (1987) has shown that the threat of future punishment can sustain a more liberal trading environment than that predicted under the static Nash equilibrium. This is supported by the United States-Japan trade friction caused by the threat of the Super 301 clause, which resulted in several concessions being made by Japan and by the negotiations under the SII talks. Accordingly, special protection is given to the U.S. semiconductor industry when the terms of trade appear to be adverse because of below-cost dumping of Japanese semiconductors in the United States and Asian markets.

However, this theory points out that terms-of-trade effects will impact national welfare only when the volume of underlying trade is high. Therefore, periods of high trade volume, such as semiconductors, telephones, digital switches, customer premises equipment, and cellular telephones traded, between the United States and Japan are likely to correspond to periods of managed trade or the incentive for it. In such a case the gains from managed trade will outweigh the losses from the Super 301 enforcement or other forms of punishment that make free trade unsustainable. Theory suggests that an approach of special protection during periods of high trade volume will prevent large-scale defection of countries from the international trade environment, reverting them to the noncooperative Nash equilibrium.

In the United States-Japan case the issue is not so much of trade volume as of trade imbalance. The continued $50 billion deficit in the trade balance led to the threat-of-punishment policy of the United States. When applied to trade imbalance, the theory of managed trade will depend on the sectoral makeup of the imbalance. If the trade imbalance widens, greater levels of protection will be mandated as the U.S. imports increase. Simultaneously the levels of protection fall in Japan as the volume of trade expands. In such an environment, managed trade correlates periods of high trade volume with increased protection, because in such periods the incentive to defect or withdraw cooperation is highest. This theory gets recognition in the GATT provisions, which provide safeguards. Under such provisions, countries can increase protection in the event of unforeseen developments. Under such circumstances, managed trade does not run counter to the multilateral free trade goals of the GATT charter.

The Uruguay Round negotiations came back on track in March 1991 "fraught with agonizing technical detail when at stake is the whole international trading system" (Ukawa 1991). The GATT charter has provided protection to the low-income countries against disagreements, and bilateral negotiations will have adverse effects on Asian countries and limit their access to world markets. Japan's imports have grown over the years. Its total imports from the rest of the world in 1990 were $234 billion, an increase of approximately 10 percent over 1989, making Japan the third largest market in the world after Europe and the United States. One-third of these imports go to Japan from the NIEs of Asia, which is twice the volume imported by Germany. The Japanese pay extra attention to the quality of their exports, which has been widely promulgated in Japan from the Deming standards of quality over the years. However, the United States believes that there is greater scope for the "internalization of the Japanese market."

"GATT's last chance" as *The Economist* (June 1, 1991) calls this phase of Uruguay Round is based on international concessions, compromise, and changing attitudes on the part of its members. The fast-track authority extended by the U.S. Congress will enable negotiations to proceed faster, but difficult issues will continue to be services, intellectual property, and agriculture. These issues will be tackled by the Group of Negotiations on Services (GNS) and Group of Negotiations on Goods.

In 1991, the U.S. Department of Commerce stated that the United States' bilateral trade deficit with Japan was $40 billion, having declined from $60 billion in 1987 and that in 1993 U.S. trade with Japan will still have a deficit. As such, new laws and revisionist policies will run counter to the spirit of GATT. Managed trade theory agrees, no matter how the volume expands in traded telecommunications equipment between the United States and Japan. While the United States demands fair trade rather than free trade, fairness is embodied in the GATT agreement in terms of its rules for nondiscrimination, reciprocity, and impartial settlement of disputes. The GATT has become a victim of its own success (Bhagwati 1991), and now its members call for a results-oriented rather than a rules-based approach. Bhagwati questions whether Japan was too efficient and grew too quickly for its competitors even though it submitted to VERs since the 1930s.

The managed trade policy is best highlighted in the semiconductors dispute between the United States and Japan. In 1991 a new Semiconductor Agreement replaced a 1986 pact. "It is an important guidepost to the future direction of the international trading system for high technology goods" (Flamm 1991). It is important because it will impact on trade in computers, satellites, telecommunications, and other high-technology equipment.

This chapter has shown the extent of mergers and joint ventures between U.S. and Japanese producers. The issue then is to what extent will such cooperative ventures render the concept of a competitive market place meaningless? Furthermore MITI's subsidies for research and development and for trade to the microchip industry stood in the way of U.S. exports to Japan, and the 1986 agreement had promised a market share of 20 percent by 1991 to imports. It has so far risen to 13 percent. It was noted previously that the 1986 agreement made it easier for the Japanese producers to garner higher profits by imposing ceilings on the production of DRAM output. The success of chip exports demonstrated the advantages of cooperation between the Japanese government and industry. The objective was to strengthen Japanese computer and supercomputers industries. Simultaneously NTT developed programs for leading edge semiconductor technology through its very large scale integration program.

The semiconductor trade scenario led the U.S. proposal at the Uruguay Round to include the concept of dumping in its new charter. Japan does not include its research and development costs at the start of the product cycle in its high-technology products but waits for the impact of the learning curve to reduce manufacturing costs. Such forward pricing has also been used by the U.S. semiconductor manufacturers. Consequently, dumping charges can be made even against U.S. suppliers, thus including this in GATT rules may be counterproductive.

In June 1991, Washington and Tokyo agreed on a new five-year accord for semiconductors. This agreement relies on the private sector to boost the U.S. share of the Japanese chip market to 20 percent or more by 1992 (*The Wall Street Journal*, June 5, 1991). Japan has promised to establish nondiscriminatory purchasing rules. In return, the United States will dismantle its monitoring system for Japanese chip makers of price and cost data. This agreement is more transparent than the 1986 one. The United States has agreed to terminate punitive duties on Japanese laptop computers, power tools, and other products. It gives better market access to both trading partners.

In March 1991, Japan made its first overture to initiate a Sixth Generation Computer by inviting companies and universities around the world to join a 10-year project for developing advanced computers for the next century. Japan also promised to change its intellectual property laws so that foreign participants can hold up to a 50 percent stake in inventions originating from this project.

It appears as if the friction cycle is getting resolved under the application of the Nash two-person cooperative game. Matsuyama's thesis (1990) that long-term protection would destroy the competitive pressures on an industry and reduce its incentives for holding down costs is being recognized by MITI and the Japanese government in their trade-liberalizing policies for the industries under review in this chapter. However, the Japanese protection of its electronics industry from the 1970s onward did not reduce their competitive power or their incentive to invest in research and development. In this respect Matsuyama's hypothesis cannot be substantiated. Although theoretically managed trade, even at a low-level of protection, may be considered as affording an optimal welfare effect, adopting such a policy would become dangerous, as was shown in the Motorola case (see Table 9.2).

In today's interdependent world, the concept of any one country gaining economic dominance or claiming superpower status is a myth, especially if the country lacks natural resources. As Michael Porter (1990) argues, competition is the basis for successful international trade. Only free trade and a level playing field will impart health to both economies and to their neighboring countries. The benefits of bilateral free trade are not additive works under all conditions. In our current high-technology world, in which research and development costs are massive, businesses want access to markets. This access can better be achieved through a multilateral trade regime like the GATT.

The telecommunications annex proposed by the United States is worth multilateral consideration because telecommunications affects other services such as banking, insurance, travel, and financial services. Even production services become more tradeable because of their heavy dependence on telecommunications. The dynamic changes in international telecommunications have blurred the difference between equipment and services. The U.S. telecommunications annex to the Agreement on Trade in Services aims at covering some of the concerns of the Organization for Economic Cooperation and Development and of developing countries in terms of access to data bases and networks. This annex was intended to be attached to the framework agreement in order to identify "the rules of the game" in international telecommunications trade, but it served the unintended role of contributing to the failure of the GATT negotiations, even though disagreement over agricultural issues was the chief cause.

The multilateral efforts of the GNS have helped industry as well as government to define telecommunications services and focus attention on their underlying tradeability. The issue on which most deliberation has taken place in the United States is whether the most-favored-nation (MFN) principles should be applied to telecommunications. Application of MFN is likely to discourage liberalization that might have otherwise taken place, because other countries will have limited incentives to open their markets. In the United States, foreign suppliers can currently enter the basic long-distance market without prior government authorization. But U.S. suppliers cannot do the same in Japan and in countries that have state-run monopolies. Consequently, the United States has demanded market access by other signatories. The application of MFN without market access guarantees would further reduce the possibility of opening markets to fair trade.

The text of the telecommunications annex has a number of brackets (meaning areas of disagreement) added by developing countries that transform the annex from a trade-liberalizing document into one that condones current restrictive practices. The United States has offered national treatment for all enhanced services provided by foreign entities and expects other countries like Japan to do the same. Instead of being "a bill of rights for users and service providers," the current telecommunications annex threatens the rights of intracorporate communications that transit transborder networks over leased lines. It has become a bill of rights for monopolistic telephone administrations that limit access, usage, and bypass. The principles of the GATT in terms of the new annex will not help corporate networks or be applied to separate satellite systems. The whole area of infrastructure is left out of the annex. In fact, the future of bilateral agreements such as the bilateral agreement between the United States and Japan for international value-added networks would become questionable if the agreement had to be applied to all countries without conditions for market access. Because less developed countries oppose conditional MFN status, the United States has withdrawn some of its opposition in this regard.

It is unclear whether the GNS will approve a complete text covering concepts, definitions, principles, and institutional aspects of telecommunications. The legally binding annex proposed by the United States has yet to be agreed on. Although switching and transmission equipment dominate trade, the fastest growing sectors are mobile and data communications, growing at 23 percent a year and 17 percent a year, respectively. Telecommunication policies will affect trade in two ways. First, they alter the operating costs of TNCs that are major users of information-based services. Second, they affect market access by determining which equipment and services can be sold under competition and which will remain under monopoly control. As Geza Feketekuty (1990) aptly pointed out, "the strategic resource in the new economy is information. The strategic infrastructure is the telecommunications system. The strategic territorial unit for organizing production is the world."

Both the United States and Japan are aware of the structural changes taking place. Both countries are making critical changes in policy to avoid open confrontation and trade war. As we say in the application of game theory, the friction cycles are getting reduced and solutions are being found on a case-by-case basis to cooperative gamesmanship. After 45 years under the U.S. security umbrella, Japan needs to take world leadership and play a stronger constructive role in the GNS and the International Telecommunications Union (ITU). Japan may have to stop looking at the world purely from an economic window and share a greater burden with other superpowers.

CONCLUSION

This analysis has shown that bilateral trade strategies between the United States and Japan were addressed outside the purview of the GATT. Trade disputes in specific telecommunications services and equipment have been analyzed within the framework of the economic theory of games. This review of game theory has advanced the analysis of the trade dispute between the United States and Japan.

The main question facing policymakers is whether the breakthrough in trade negotiations since April 1990 will work in the future. Japan has agreed to tighten its antitrust laws. The promotion of structural reforms in Japan will provide a stimulus to improved trade relations. Case-by-case trade reciprocity is being established in an effort to establish a level playing field. In most cases, Japan has made concessions and reduced the friction cycle. It has been removed from the Super 301 clause. These changes may not reduce the trade imbalance but they provide a new framework for the two countries to jointly deal with global concerns within the GATT and the ITU. Much will depend on how Japan develops a world view to complement its trade surplus. With scant natural resources, Japan needs free trade as much, if not more, than the United States does. Their economies are interdependent and interlinked, and the general perception of unfairness needs to be dispelled. In a world of shared power relationships, leadership must come from both countries to enable the information age to spread pluralistic democracy.

APPENDIX: DEFINITIONS OF GAME THEORY TERMS USED IN TEXT

We provide the following brief definitions to assist the reader. More formal definitions can be found in Schotter and Schwodiauer (1980) and a variety of other sources.

Cooperative and noncooperative games: A cooperative game is one in which the players may communicate with one another and make enforceable agreements. In noncooperative games, such communication and agreements are not available.

Imputation: An imputation is a payoff vector in which each player obtains at least the amount he might achieve without cooperation with other players or coalitions of players and which exhausts the total value of the game.

Dominate strategies: A strategy (S^a_i) and its solution for player i dominate another strategy (say S^b_i) when the payoff to player i is greater under a than under b.

Objection and counterobjection: An objection to imputation x arises when a player can find an imputation y that provides him with a higher payoff than that obtainable from x. A counterobjection results form another player finding an imputation z with higher payoffs than either x or y. An objection is justified if there is no counterobjection to it.

Core: The core is the set of all imputations that are not dominated by any player or coalition. (It is important to realize that the converse is not necessarily true: there may be imputations outside the core that are not dominated by those within it.)

Bargaining set: Those imputations against which no player or coalition has a justifiable objection.

Nash solution: A Nash solution (also called a noncooperative equilibrium) arises from noncooperative bargaining if there is full revelation of preferences by all players at each stage. It is the basic solution concept for noncooperative games.

Strategy: The aggregation of a player's moves in such a sequential game is called a strategy, and a game that consists of possibly an infinite number of rounds is called a supergame.

Two-person, zero-sum games: Those games for which the gains for one player always exactly offset the losses of the other. These games are also known as strictly competitive games.

REFERENCES

Aronson, J. and P. Cowhey. 1988. *When Countries Talk*. Cambridge, MA: Ballinger.

Bagwell, Kyle and Robert Staiger. 1990. "A Theory of Managed Trade." *American Economic Review*, Vol. 80: 4, pp. 779–90.

Bhagwati, J. 1991. *The World Trading System at Risk*. New York: Harvester Wheatsheet.

Binmore, K. and P. Dasgupta, eds. 1987. "Nash Bargaining Theory: An Introduction." In *The Economics of Bargaining*, pp. 1–26. New York: Blackwell.

Chan, Kenneth. 1988. "Trade Negotiations in a Nash Bargaining Model," *Journal of International Economics*, Vol. 25, pp. 353–63.

Chandler, Alfred. 1990. *Scale and Scope*. Cambridge, MA: Harvard University Press.

Dixit, Avinash. 1987. "Strategic Aspects of Trade Theory." In *Advances in Economic Theory*, edited by Truman Bewley, pp. 329–62. Cambridge, MA: Cambridge University Press.

Emmott, William. 1989. *The Sun Also Sets: The Limits to Japan's Economic Power* London: Times Books.

Feketekuty, Geza. 1990. "New Trade Dimensions in Telecom Services," *TDR*, January, pp. 9–10.

Feldstein, Martin. 1990. "Japan's Latest Import Promotion Plan," *Wall Street Journal*, January 27.

Flamm, Kenneth. 1991. "Making New Rules: High Tech Trade Friction and the Semiconductor Industry," *The Brookings Review*, Spring, pp. 22–29.

Freidman, J. W. 1986. *Game Theory with Applications to Economics*. New York: Oxford University Press.

Hurwicz, Leonid. 1972. "On Informationally Decentralized Systems." In *Decision and Organization*, edited by McGuire and Radner, pp. 297–336. Westport: North Holland.

Ishihara, Shintaro. 1989. "The Japan That Can Say No," *Time*, November 20.

Jussawalla, Meheroo. 1987. "The Race for Telecommunications Technology: U.S. versus Japan," *Telecommunications Policy*, September.

Matsuyama, Kiminori. 1990. "Perfect Equilibria in a Trade Liberalization Game," *American Economic Review*, June, pp. 480–92.

Nash, John. 1953. "Two-Person Cooperative Games," *Econometrica*, 21, pp. 129–40.

Ohmae, Kenichi. 1990. *Borderless World*. New York: Harper.

Porter, Michael. 1990. *The Competitive Advantage of Nations*. New York: Free Press.

Roth, Alvin E. 1979. *Axiomatic Models of Bargaining*. Berlin: Springer Verlag.

Rubenstein, Arthur. 1980. "Perfect Equilibrium in a Bargaining Model," *Econometrica*, 50: 97–109.

Schotter, Andrew and G. Schwodiauer. 1980. "Economics and the Theory of Games: A Survey," *Journal of Economic Literature*, vol. 18, June, pp. 479–527.

Shubik, Martin. 1959. "Edgeworth Market Games." In *Annals of Mathematics Studies*, vol. 40, pp. 267–78. Princeton, NJ: Princeton University Press.

Ukawa, Hidetoshi. 1991. "Reactions in Japan: The International Orientation of Domestic Policies." Remarks at the Chatham House Conference, London, March 8.

____. 1991. Speech cited in *Transborder Data Report*.

von Neumann and Morgenstern. 1944. *Theory of Games and Economic Behavior*. Princeton, NJ: Princeton University Press.

Wilson, Robert. 1985. "Reputations in Games and Markets." In *Game Theoretic Models of Bargaining*, edited by Alvin E. Roth, pp. 27–62. New York: Cambridge University Press.

Index

About the Contributors

Jonathan Aronson is professor in the School of International Relations and in the Anneberg School of Communications at the University of Southern California.

Yale Braunstein is professor of economics at the Graduate School of Library Studies, University of California at Berkeley.

Douglas A. Conn is associate director of the Columbia Institute for Tele-Information and associate professor of telecommunications at the Center for Information Technology, Columbia University.

Joseph Doherty is a systems analyst and consultant for research at INSPRA Inc., in Virginia.

Fumiko Mori Halloran was a political analyst at the Japan Economic Institute from 1977 to 1983 and is now a novelist and freelance journalist who writes for newspapers and journals in Japan.

Meheroo Jussawalla is a research associate and economist at the East-West Center's Program on Communication and Journalism, Honolulu, Hawaii.

Shinzo Kobori is an economist in the research department of C. Itoh and Co. Ltd., Tokyo, Japan.

Hajime Oniki is director of the Institute for Social and Economic Research at the University of Osaka in Japan.

Barbara Ross-Pfeiffer is a doctoral candidate in economics at the University of Hawaii and a project assistant in the East-West Center's Program on Communication and Journalism, Honolulu, Hawaii.

Marcellus S. Snow is professor of economics at the University of Hawaii and chair of Graduate Studies.